The American Revolutionary Series

THE LOYALIST LIBRARY

*The American Revolutionary Series
is published in cooperation with
The Boston Public Library*

Massachusettensis

Letters to the Inhabitants of the
Province of Massachusetts-Bay

12 December, 1774–3 April, 1775

By
DANIEL LEONARD

With a New Introduction and Preface by
GEORGE ATHAN BILLIAS

GREGG PRESS
Boston 1972

This is a complete photographic reprint of a work
first published anonymously in Boston in 1775.
Reproduced from microfilm of an original copy in
The New York Public Library,
Astor, Lenox and Tilden Foundations.

First Gregg Press edition published 1972.

Printed on permanent/durable acid-free paper in
The United States of America.

973.31
L581m

Library of Congress Cataloging in Publication Data

Leonard, Daniel, 1740-1829.
    Massachusettensis.

    (American Revolutionary series)
    Reprint of the 1776 ed. with a new series, introd.,
and a pref. by G. A. Billias.   74-8538
    1. United States—Politics and government—Revolu-
tion. 2. Massachusetts—Politics and government—
Revolution. I. Title. II. Series.
E211.L57   1972   973.3'11   72-10246
ISBN 0-8398-1180-2

THE LOYALIST LIBRARY

THE LOYALISTS in the American Revolu-
tion represent one of the most misunderstood groups in our
nation's history. For the past two centuries, they have
fared badly at the hands of historians; Tories have either
been neglected, or protrayed in an unsympathetic light by
ultra-patriotic writers. The remark that a Loyalist was "a
thing whose head is in England . . . body . . . in America,
and its neck ought to be stretched," typifies the common
attitude during the first century after the Revolution. This
early period was one of outspoken nationalism, and resent-
ment against the Loyalists and former mother country
remained high. Although Anglo-American animosities
diminished in the second century, and scholars adopted a
more detached approach, the Tories were studied only
sporadically. The present collection—called the Loyalist
Library—contains both writings of important Tories and
scholarly monographs on the subject. It should help to
stimulate renewed research and interest in this forgotten
part of America's past.

History is usually written by winners, not losers, and
therefore we do not know as much about the Loyalists as
we should. For one thing, we do not know how many
Tories there actually were. The old estimate—mistakenly
attributed to John Adams—claimed that the country was
split three ways during the war: one-third becoming

Loyalists; one-third supporting the patriot cause; and one-third remaining neutral or indifferent. Modern scholars estimate that the Tories comprised something closer to nineteen percent of the total number of white Americans. Several studies included in this collection, such as Otis G. Hammond's *Tories of New Hampshire,* and Janet B. Johnson's biography of Robert Alexander, a Maryland Loyalist, provide evidence that casts serious doubts on the older assumption.

The Loyalist Library should help to correct another misconception—the idea that Tories came mainly from the upper class—from the ranks of royal officeholders, rich merchants, professional men, and well-to-do Anglicans. Recent research into the socio-economic background of Tories reveals that they hailed instead from the middle or lower classes in most of the colonies. Farmers, artisans, and small businessmen formed the backbone of the Loyalist movement for the most part. Wilbur H. Siebert's work on *The Loyalists of Pennsylvania,* for example, shows that in the Quaker colony many frontier farmers became Tories.

In geographical terms, the Loyalists were scattered throughout all of the original thirteen colonies. Virginia and Massachusetts had the smallest number. The strongest Tory support seems to have been in certain of the Middle Colonies—New York, New Jersey, and Pennsylvania—and in the South—in the Carolinas and Georgia. State studies of these areas, such as Edward Alfred Jones' *The Loyalists of New Jersey* and Harold B. Hancock's *The Delaware Loyalists,* tell us specifically who the Tories were—their names, place of residence, occupation or profession, and religion. Loyalists, moreover, tended to concentrate in urban areas and along the seacoast—except in New York, North Carolina, and parts of Pennsylvania where major pockets of Tories could be found in the interior. The treatment that Tories received at the hands of the Whigs in such seacoast cities as Boston may be gleaned from Arthur W. Eaton's biography of Mather Byles.

The Loyalist Library also provides proof that the Floridas and Nova Scotia—none of which rebelled—may have held the highest ratio of Tories. Wilbur H. Siebert's *Loyalists in East Florida, 1774 to 1785* indicates that the number of Tories in that colony increased substantially as a result of the exodus from the Carolinas and Georgia. The papers of Edward Winslow reflect the problems that incoming Loyalists encountered in resettling in Nova Scotia.

It is estimated that seventy-five to eighty thousand Loyalists left the United States during the war for England, Canada, the West Indies, and other parts of the British empire. Pamphlets of refugees like Joseph Galloway, which are reprinted here, reveal much about the views of the Loyalists who went to England. Some individuals remained men without a country, and lived out their days in London while dreaming about America. Others took up careers on the continent, as is evident in George E. Ellis' *Memoir of Sir Benjamin Thompson, Count Rumford*. Another major group—the United Empire Loyalists—whose story is presented in certain of these writings, settled in Canada and became the founding fathers of new communities.

The Loyalist Library includes also valuable primary source materials. Loyalist letters, pamphlets, and personal narratives help to shed light on the key question: Why did the American Tories remain loyal to their King? Prominent Loyalists like Daniel Leonard of Massachusetts and Joseph Galloway of Pennsylvania explain their political position in their writings. They tell us what they considered to be the proper relationship between colonies and mother country, the King and his subjects, and colonial governors and the American people. Until we view the Loyalists as men with "positive political ideas" and individuals capable of "creative statesmanship," a balanced interpretation of the Revolution will elude us, says one historian.

The Loyalist Library, then, is a combination of primary source documents and secondary materials. It includes private letters, diaries, and narratives, Tory histories and pamphlets, as well as scholarly books written on the subject. The collection makes available certain sources that were heretofore less accessible, and it should enable students to become more familiar with the Loyalist side of the story of the Revolution.

PREFACE

DANIEL LEONARD (1740-1829) a Taunton lawyer, signed himself "Massachusettensis" when he published a series of articles in the *Massachusetts Gazette* in 1774-1775. His pseudonym was intended to convey the impression that the author had deep roots in the Bay Colony. Such was the case, for Leonard's ancestry stretched back to the seventeenth century. He sprang from a prominent Massachusetts family whose fortune was made in producing iron. Politically they were so powerful in Bristol county that it was once called "the land of the Leonards."

Leonard was himself one of the Bay Colony's leading politicians. Graduating from Harvard in 1764, he studied law in the office of his future father-in-law, who was speaker in the House of Representatives at one time. Although favoring the Whigs at first, Leonard was converted to the Loyalist cause by Thomas Hutchinson. When the British appointed royal councillors for Massachusetts in 1774, Leonard was named as one. His acceptance of the post annoyed his neighbors, and he was soon forced to flee to Boston to seek protection of the redcoats. Leonard lost his property and citizenship when he sailed from Boston with the British army in 1776. After the Revolution he became Chief Justice of Bermuda, and later, as a London lawyer, was regarded as "dean of English barristers."

Leonard's "Massachusettensis" articles read like a

lawyer's brief. His thesis is that self-serving Whig politicians were primarily responsible for the turmoil within the Bay Colony. He accused them of establishing a democratic despotism. The Massachusetts Whigs instead of fighting for the traditional rights of Englishmen were leading America down the road to rebellion and independence. Britain, as far as he was concerned, had acted within her rightful powers during the constitutional crisis. Leonard's legal training is evident in his impressive use of constitutional and historical precedents to support his case.

Leonard's articles were answered by another lawyer— John Adams. Using the nom de plum "Novanglus"—or New Englishman—Adams challenged Leonard's points one-by-one as though the two men were arguing in court. Adams presented a sympathetic view of the Whigs, and a different picture of the British constitution, imperial relationship, and colonial social structure.

"Massachusettensis" represents the Loyalist case in its legal dimensions. Leonard's articles and Adams' replies constitute one of the most important exchanges between Tories and Whigs on Constitutional matters in the pre-Revolutionary period.

George Athan Billias
Clark University

Maſſachuſettenſis.

[Price, TWO SHILLINGS.]

Massachusettensis:

OR

A SERIES of LETTERS,

CONTAINING

A FAITHFUL STATE OF MANY IMPORTANT
AND STRIKING FACTS,

WHICH LAID THE FOUNDATION OF THE

PRESENT TROUBLES

IN THE

Province of the *Massachusetts-Bay*;

INTERSPERSED WITH

ANIMADVERSIONS and REFLECTIONS,

ORIGINALLY

Addreſſed to the PEOPLE of that Province, and worthy the
Conſideration of the TRUE PATRIOTS of this Country.

By a PERSON of Honor upon the Spot.

Falſus Honor juvat, & mendax Infamia terret,
Quem, niſi mendoſum & mendacem? Vir bonus eſt quis?
Qui Conſulta Patrum, qui Leges Juraque ſervat.
HOR. Ep. xvi.

BOSTON printed:
LONDON reprinted for J. MATHEWS, No. 18, in the *Strand*,
MDCCLXXVI.

PREFACE.

THIS excellent pamphlet was publifhed in a feries of letters, which firft appeared in one of the weekly news-papers at Bofton, and afterwards in the form of a pamphlet, entitled MASSACHUSETTENSIS, in the courfe of the laft winter. It has been thought, that a republication of a detail and difcuffion of facts and circumftances, which were unanfwerable upon the fpot, might at leaft filence the clamors of thofe people at home, who, without proper evidence or information, but with an excefs of terror for our public liberties, have perfuaded themfelves, that the caufe of America and true patriotifm is one and the fame, and that, therefore, the conftitution of this country muft at all events fubmit to the ruinous pretenfions of her colonies. To enlarge upon the merits of the piece itfelf, either refpecting the intimate knowledge it contains of the fubject, or the force, acumen and juftice of the author's reafonings (whatever room the editor may fuppofe there is for encomiums), is purpofely omitted, in deference to the public, who will undoubtedly render the approbation it may be found to deferve. It is neceffary,

fary, and only neceffary, to fay, that thefe letters' were written by a gentleman of honor, rank and learning, who faw what he defcribes, and who knows the truth of what he avers. The reflections, which he has made (and reflections, juftly made, conftitute, as M. *Rollin* obferves, " the very foul " of hiftory"), are natural and folid deductions from the ftate of things under his own obfervation. They need only a candid and impartial perufal to be both admitted and admired; though, to the difgrace of human nature, it muft be owned, in the words of a very ingenious writer, that *weak is the effect of eloquence* (and, I may add, even of reafon and truth itfelf) *on the prædeterminations of party**. In a word, his facts and arguments not only feem inconteftable; but there appears, throughout the whole, that fpirit of philanthropy and concern for the welfare of his mifguided countrymen, which recommends the author as much to the heart, as his good fenfe does his book to the underftanding.

The reader, however, ought to be apprized of the author's meaning in the ufe of the words Whig and Tory, which frequently occur in the letters. Thefe terms have very different fignifications in Old and New England. In America, the word TORY now implies *a friend to the fupremacy of the Britifh conftitution over all the empire*; and the word WHIG, *an afferter of colonial independence*, or (what is juft the fame) of legiflations, diftinct and divided from Britifh legiflation, in all the feveral provinces. In this fenfe, and in this fenfe alone, are the terms

applied

---

* Principles of Penal Law. c. v.

applied throughout the letters (as the author himfelf explains them at page 115.), and have no fort
of reference to the odious diftinctions which formerly prevailed, but have now happily fubfided,
in this country, upon the notion of a *feparate* intereft between the *King* and *People*. In the prefent
controverfy, the King and People of the Britifh
iflands have, and can have, but *one* intereft; which
American independence, aiming firft at the *unity* of
our conftitution, then at the *extent* of our commerce, and laftly at the *dignity* of our power, attempts to deftroy. Yet this is the mock-patriot-
ifm of the day—a patriotifm, founded on the ignorance of fome, urged by the artifices of others, and
tending to the ruin of all. To be a patriot in
mode, is to aim at a feparation of the ftate into
twenty or *thirty* different parcels, inftead of feeking
a confolidation of feveral provinces into *one* empire.
People of this ftamp are for faving our enemies the
trouble of enforcing the difficult part of their motto
— *divide & impera* — by attempting the *firft* for
them. Happily, the good fenfe of the nation has
begun to detect the impofture; and, 'tis hoped,
that, in a little time, the well-difpofed Americans
will perceive, that Britons, detefting tyranny in all
its forms, and always willing to refcue even foreign
nations from the yoke of bondage, have no
thoughts of impofing it upon their children. 'They
have ever been too brave to be flaves themfelves,
and too generous to make flaves of others. They
never had more liberty in their perfons, properties,
religion, fpeech, writings, and actions, than in the
prefent reign: I had almoft faid, they cannot have
more, without an abrogation of all order and go-
vern-

vernment. Thefe invaluable bleffings can only be fecured by the prefervation of their happy conftitution. In a word, let their enemies name the monarchy or republic upon earth, which can boaft their noble zeal for true liberty, or an equal pof-feffion of public freedom !

And what has America obtained by her revolt from the conftitution of Britain ? I fpeak not of that province, which is at prefent the feat of war; but of thofe, who are yet unmolefted in the exercife of their new prerogatives, and of their boafted *natural rights*. What oppreffions have not thefe endured from the arbitrary dictates of a lawlefs congrefs, or the favage determinations of an infolent mob ? Peaceable fubjects, merely for being *peaceable*, have been haled away to prifon, forced into their army, or ftripped of their poffeffions. Men, who have remonftrated againft fuch brutal proceedings, have been ftill more ignominioufly treated, and, without either the appearance of legal decifion or the forms of legal punifhment, have been expofed to all the indecent refentments of an abandoned multitude. Clergymen, of the eftablifhed church, have been driven from their cures, upon no other account than for not omitting the prayer for the King and royal family, in the common ufe of divine fervice. Thefe are fome of the choiceft bleffings, which congreffes and committees have beftowed : Let me afk, if fuch can poffibly be expected from the King and parliament of Great-Britain ?

L E T T E R   I.

To the Inhabitants of the Province of the Maſſachu-ſetts-Bay.

WHEN a people, by what means ſoever, are reduced to ſuch a ſituation, that every thing they hold dear, as men and citizens, is at ſtake, it is not only excuſable, but even praiſeworthy, for an individual to offer to the public any thing, that he may think has a tendency to ward off the impending danger; nor ſhould he be reſtrained from an apprehenſion that what he may offer will be unpopular, any more than a phyſician ſhould be reſtrained from preſcribing a ſalutary medicine, through fear it might be unpalatable to his patient.

The preſs, when open to all parties and influenced by none, is a ſalutary engine in a free ſtate, perhaps a neceſſary one to preſerve the freedom of that ſtate; but, when a party has gained the aſcendency ſo far as to become the licenſers of the preſs, either by an act of government, or by playing off the reſentment of the populace againſt printers and authors; the preſs itſelf becomes an engine of oppreſſion or licentiouſneſs, and is as pernicious to ſociety as otherwiſe it would be beneficial. It is too true to be denied, that, ever ſince the origin of our controverſy with Great Britain, the preſs, in this town, has been much devoted to the partizans of liberty: they have been indulged in publiſhing what they pleaſed, *fas vel nefas*, while little has been publiſhed on the part of government. The effect this muſt have had upon the minds of the people in general is obvious; they muſt have formed their opinion upon a partial view of the ſubject, and of courſe it muſt have been in ſome degree erroneous: In ſhort, the changes

have

have been rung fo often upon oppreffion, tyranny and
flavery, that, whether fleeping or waking, they are continually vibrating in our ears; and it is now high time to
afk ourfelves, whether we have not been deluded by found
only.

My dear countrymen, let us diveft ourfelves of prejudice,
take a view of our prefent wretched fituation, contraft it
with our former happy one, carefully inveftigate the caufe,
and induftrioufly feek fome means to efcape the evils we
now feel, and prevent thofe that we have reafon to expect.

We have been fo long advancing to our prefent ftate, and
by fuch gradations, that perhaps many of us are infenfible
of our true ftate and real danger. Should you be told,
that acts of high treafon are flagrant through the country,
that a great part of the province is in actual rebellion; would
you believe it true? Should you not deem the perfon affert-
ing it an enemy to the province? Nay, fhould you not
fpurn him from you with indignation? Be calm, my
friends, it is neceffary to know the worft of a difeafe, to
enable us to provide an effectual remedy. Are not the
bands of fociety cut afunder, and the fanctions, that hold
man to man, trampled upon? Can any of us recover a
debt, or obtain compenfation for an injury, by law? Are
not many perfons, whom once we refpected and revered,
driven from their homes and families, and forced to fly to
the army for protection, for no other reafon but their having accepted commiffions under our king? Is not civil
government diffolved? Some have been made to believe,
that nothing fhort of attempting the life of the king, or
fighting his troops, can amount to high treafon or rebellion. If, reader, you are one of thofe, apply to an honeft
lawyer (if fuch an one can be found), and enquire what
kind of offence it is, for a number of men to affemble
armed, and forceably to obftruct the courfe of juftice, even
to prevent the king's courts from being held at their ftated
terms; for a body of people to feize upon the king's provincial revenue, I mean the monies collected by virtue of
grants made to his Majefty for the fupport of his government within this province; for a body of men to affemble
without

without being called by authority, and to pass governmental acts; or for a number of people to take the militia out of the hands of the king's representative; or to form a new militia, or to raise men and appoint officers for a public purpose, without the order or permission of the king or his representative; or for a number of men to take to their arms, and march with a professed design of opposing the king's troops: ask, reader, of such a lawyer, what is the crime, and what the punishment; and if per chance thou art one that hast been active in these things, and art not insensibility itself, his answer will harrow up thy soul.

I assure you, my friends, I would not that this conduct should be told beyond the borders of this province; I wish it were consigned to perpetual oblivion; but, alas, it is too notorious to be concealed: our news-papers have already published it to the world, and we can neither prevent nor conceal it. The shaft is already sped, and the utmost exertion is necessary to prevent the blow. We already feel the effects of anarchy: mutual confidence, affection and tranquillity, those sweeteners of human life, are succeeded by distrust, hatred and wild uproar; the useful arts of agriculture and commerce are neglected for cabaling, mobbing this or the other man, because he acts, speaks, or is suspected of thinking different from the prevailing sentiment of the times, in purchasing arms and forming a militia, O height of madness! with a professed design of opposing Great-Britain. I suspect many of us have been induced to join in these measures, or but faintly to oppose them, from an apprehension that Great-Britain would not or could not exert herself sufficiently to subdue America. Let us consider this matter: However closely we may hug ourselves in the opinion that the parliament has no right to tax or legislate for us, the people of England hold the contrary opinion as firmly: they tell us we are a part of the British empire; that every state from the nature of government must have a supreme uncontroulable power coëxtensive with the empire itself; and that, that power is vested in parliament. It is as absurd to deny this doctrine in Great-Britain, as it is to assert it in the

colonies;

colonies; fo there is but little probability of ferving ourfelves at this day by our ingenious diftinctions between a
right of legiflature for one purpofe and not for another.
We have bid them defiance, and the longeft fword muft
carry it, unlefs we change our meafures. Mankind are the
fame in all parts of the world; the fame fondnefs for dominion that prefides in the breaft of an American, actuates
the breaft of an European. If the colonies are not a part
of the Britifh empire already, and fubject to the fupreme
authority of the ftate, Great-Britain will make them fo.
Had we been prudent enough to confine our oppofition
within certain limits, we might have ftood fome chance of
fucceeding once more; but alas we have paffed the Rubi-
con. It is now univerfally faid and believed, in England,
that if this opportunity of reclaiming the colonies, and reducing them to a fenfe of their duty is loft, they in truth
will be difmembered from the empire, and become as diftinct a ftate from Great-Britain as Hanover; that is, although they may continue their allegiance to the perfon of
the King, they will own none to the imperial crown of
Great-Britain, nor yield obedience to any of her laws but
fuch as they fhall think proper to adopt. Can you indulge
the thought one moment, that Great-Britain will confent
to this? For what has fhe protected and defended the colonies againft the maritime powers of Europe, from their firft
Britifh fettlement to this day? For what did fhe purchafe
New-York of the Dutch? For what was fhe fo lavifh of her
beft blood and treafure in the conqueft of Canada, and other
territories in America? Was it to raife up a rival ftate, or
to enlarge her own empire? Or, if the confideration of
empire was out of the queftion, what fecurity can fhe have
of our trade, when once fhe has loft our obedience? I mention thefe things, my friends, that you may know how
people reafon upon the fubject in England; and to convince
you that you are much deceived, if you imagine that Great-
Britain will accede to the claims of the colonies: fhe will as
foon conquer New-England as Ireland or Canada, if either
of them revolted; and by arms, if the milder influences
of government prove ineffectual. Perhaps you are as fa-
tally

tally miftaken in another refpect, I mean as to the power
of Great-Britain to conquer; but can any of you, that
think foberly upon the matter, be fo deluded as to believe
that Great-Britain, who fo lately carried her arms with
fuccefs to every part of the globe, triumphed over the
united powers of France and Spain, and whofe fleets give
law to the ocean, is unable to conquer us? Should the
colonies unite in a war with Great-Britain (which by the
way is not a fuppofable cafe) the colonies fouth of Pennfylvania would be unable to furnifh any men ; they have
not more than is neceffary to govern their numerous flaves,
and to defend themfelves againft the Indians. I will fuppofe that the northern colonies can furnifh as many, and
indeed more men than can be ufed to advantage; but have
you arms fit for a campaign? If you have arms, have
you military ftores, or can you procure them? When
this war is proclaimed, all fupplies from foreign parts
will be cut off. Have you money to maintain the war?
Or had you all thofe things, fome others are ftill wanting,
which are abfolutely neceffary to encounter regular troops,
that is difcipline, and that fubordination whereby each
can command all below him from a general officer to
the loweft fubaltern : thefe you neither have nor can
have in fuch a war. It is well known that the provincials
in the late war were never brought to a proper difcipline,
though they had the example of the regular troops to en-
courage, and the martial law to enforce it. We all know,
notwithftanding the province law for regulating the militia,
it was under but little more command than what the officers
could obtain from treating and humouring the common
foldiers : what then can be expected from fuch an army as
you will bring into the field, if you bring any, each one a
politician, puffed up with his own opinion, and feeling
himfelf fecond to none? Can any of you command ten
thoufand fuch men? Can you punifh the difobedient?
Can all your wifdom direct their ftrength, courage and
activity to any given point? Would not the leaft difappointment or unfavourable afpect caufe a general derelic-
tion of the fervice? Your new-fangled militia have already
given

given us a *specimen* of their future conduct. In some of
their companies, they have already chosen two, in others
three sets of officers, and are as dissatisfied with the last
choice as the first. I do not doubt the natural bravery of
my countrymen : all men would act the same part in the
same situation. Such is the army, with which you are' to
oppose the most powerful nation upon the globe. An
experienced officer would rather take his chance with five
thousand British troops, than with fifty thousand such militia. I have hitherto confined my observations to the war
within the interior parts of the colonies ; let us now turn
our eyes to our extensive sea coast, and that we find
wholly at the mercy of Great-Britain ; our trade, fishery,
navigation and maritime towns taken from us, the very day
that war is proclaimed. Inconceivably shocking the scene,
if we turn our views to the wilderness; our back settlements
a prey to our ancient enemy, the Canadians, whose wounds
received from us in the late war will bleed afresh at the
prospect of revenge, and to the numerous tribes of savages, whose tender mercies are cruelties : thus with the
British navy in the front, Canadians and savages in the
rear, a regular army in the midst, we must be certain that,
when ever the sword of civil war is unsheathed, devasta-
tion will pass through our land like a whirlwind, our
houses be burnt to ashes, our fair possessions laid waste,
and he that falls by the sword will be happy in escaping
a more ignominious death.

I have hitherto gone upon a supposition that all the colonies from Nova-Scotia to Georgia would unite in the war
against Great-Britain ; but I believe if we consider coolly
upon the matter, we shall find no reason to expect any af-
sistance out of New-England : if so, there will be no arm
stretched out to save us, New-England, or perhaps this
self-devoted province will fall alone the unpitied victim of
its own folly, and furnish the world with one more instance
of the fatal consequences of rebellion.

I have as yet said nothing of the difference in sentiment among ourselves : upon a superficial view we
might imagine, that this province was nearly unanimous,
but

but the cafe is far different. A very confiderable part of the men of property in this province are at this day firmly attached to the caufe of government; bodies of men compelling perfons to difavow their fentiments, to refign commiffions, or to fubfcribe leagues and covenants, have wrought no change in their fentiments : it has only attached them more clofely to government, and caufed them to wifh more fervently, and to pray more devoutly for its reftoration: thefe and thoufands befide, if they fight at all, will fight under the banners of loyalty. I can affure you that affociations are now forming in feveral parts of this province for the fupport of his Majefty's government and mutual defence; and let me tell you, when ever the royal ftandard fhall be fet up, there will be fuch a flocking to it, as will aftonifh the moft obdurate. And now, in God's name, what is it that has brought us to this brink of deftruction ? Has not the government of Great-Britain been as mild and equitable in the colonies as in any part of her extenfive dominions ? Has not fhe been a nurfing mother to us from the days of our infancy to this time ? Has fhe not been indulgent almoft to a fault ? Might not each one of us at this day have fat quietly under his own vine and fig-tree, and there have been none to make us afraid, were it not for our own folly ? Will not pofterity be amazed, when they are told that the prefent diftraction took its rife from a three-penny duty on tea, and call it a more unaccountable frenzy, and more difgraceful to the annals of America than that of the *witchcraft*.

I will attempt in the next paper to retrace the fteps and mark the progreffions that led us to this ftate. I promife to do it with fidelity, and, if any thing fhould look like reflecting on individuals or bodies of men, it muft be fet down to my impartiality, and not to a fondnefs for cenfuring.

MASSACHUSETTENSIS.

December 12, 1774.

LET-

L E T T E R   II.

To the Inhabitants of the Province of Maſſachuſetts-Bay.

My dear Countrymen,

I ENDEAVOURED laſt week to convince you of our real danger, not to render you deſperate, but to induce you to ſeek immediately ſome effectual remedy. Our caſe is not remedileſs, as we have to deal with a nation not leſs generous and humane than powerful and brave; juſt indeed, but not vindictive.

I ſhall, in this and ſucceſſive papers, trace this yet growing diſtemper through its ſeveral ſtages, from its firſt riſe to the preſent hour, point out the cauſes, mark the effects, ſhew the madneſs of perſevering in our preſent line of conduct, and recommend what, I have been long convinced, is our only remedy. I confeſs my ſelf to be one of thoſe that think our preſent calamity is in a great meaſure to be attributed to the bad policy of a popular party in this province; and that their meaſures for ſeveral years paſt, whatever may have been their intention, have been diametrically oppoſite to their profeſſion,—the public good; and cannot, at preſent, but compare their leaders to a falſe guide, who, having led a benighted traveller through many mazes and windings in a thick wood, finds himſelf at length on the brink of a horrid precipice, and, to ſave himſelf, ſeizes faſt hold of his follower, to the utmoſt hazard of plunging both headlong down the ſteep, and being daſhed in pieces together againſt the rocks below.

In ordinary caſes, we may talk in the meaſured language of a courtier; but when ſuch a weight of vengeance is ſuſpended over our heads, by a ſingle thread, as threatens every moment to cruſh us to atoms, delicacy itſelf would be ill-timed: I will declare the plain truth whenever I find it, and claim it as a right to canvaſs popular meaſures and expoſe their errors and pernicious tendency, as freely as governmental meaſures are canvaſſed, ſo long as I confine myſelf within the limits of the law.

At the concluſion of the late war, Great-Britain found, that, though ſhe had humbled her enemies, and greatly enlarged

larged her own empire, that the national debt amounted
to almoft one hundred and fifty millions, and that the annual expence of keeping her extended dominions in a ftate
of defence, which good policy dictates no lefs in a time of
peace than war, was increafed in proportion to the new ac-
quifitions. Heavy taxes and duties were already laid, not
only upon the luxuries and conveniences, but even the neceffaries of life in Great-Britain and Ireland. She knew,
that the colonies were as much benefited by the conquefts
in the late war, as any part of the empire, and indeed
more fo, as their continental foes were fubdued, and they
might now extend their fettlements not only to Canada,
but even to the weftern ocean—The greateft opening was
given to agriculture, the natural livelihood of the country,
that ever was known in the hiftory of the world, and their
trade was protected by the Britifh navy. The revenue to
the crown, from America, amounted to but little more
than the charges of collecting it.—She thought it as reafonable, that the colonies fhould bear a part of the national
burden, as that they fhould fhare in the national benefit.
For this purpofe, the ftamp-act was paffed. The colonies
foon found, that the duties impofed by the ftamp-act would
be grievous, as they were laid upon cuftom-houfe papers,
law-proceedings, conveyancing, and indeed extended to
almoft all their internal trade and dealings. It was generally believed through the colonies, that this was a tax not
only exceeding our proportion, but beyond our utmoft
ability to pay. This idea united the colonies generally
in oppofing it. At firft we did not dream of denying the
authority of parliament to tax us, much lefs to legiflate
for us. We had always confidered ourfelves, as a part of
the Britifh empire, and the parliament, as the fupreme
legiflature of the whole. Acts of parliament for regulating
our internal polity were familiar. We had paid poftage,
agreeable to act of parliament for eftablifhing a poft-office,
duties impofed for regulating trade, and even for raifing a
revenue to the crown, without queftioning the right, though
we clofely adverted to the rate or quantum. We knew that,
in all thofe acts of government, the good of the whole had

C   been

been confulted, and, whenever through want of information any thing grievous had been ordained, we were fure of obtaining redrefs by a proper reprefentation of it. We were happy in our fubordination ; but in an evil hour, under the influence of fome malignant planet, the defign was formed of oppofing the ftamp-act by a denial of the right of parliament to make it. The love of empire is fo predominant in the human breaft, that we *rarely* find an individual content with relinquifhing a power that he is able to retain ; *never*, a body of men. Some few months after it was known that the ftamp-act was paffed, fome refolves of the houfe of burgeffes in Virginia, denying the right of parliament to tax the colonies, made their appearance. We read them with wonder—they favoured of independence—they flattered the human paffions—the reafoning was fpecious—we wifhed it conclufive. The tranfition, to believing it fo, was eafy—and we, and almoft all America, followed their example, in refolving that the parliament had no fuch right. It now became unpopular to fuggeft the contrary ; his life would be in danger that afferted it. The news-papers were open to but one fide of the queftion; and the inflammatory pieces that iffued weekly from the prefs, worked up the populace to a fit temper to commit the outrages that infued. A non-importation was agreed upon, which alarmed the merchants and manufacturers in England. It was novel, and the people in England then fuppofed, that the love of liberty was fo powerful in an American merchant, as to ftifle his love of gain, and that the agreement would be religioufly adhered to. It has been faid, that feveral thoufands were expended in England, to foment the difturbances there. However that may be, oppofition to the miniftry was then gaining ground, from circumftances, foreign to this.— The miniftry was changed, and the ftamp-act repealed.— The repealing ftatute paffed, with difficulty however, through the houfe of peers : near forty noble lords protefted againft giving way to fuch an oppofition, and foretold what has fince literally come to pafs in confequence of it. When the ftatute was made, impofing duties upon glafs, paper,

India

India teas, &c. imported into the colonies, it was said, that this was another instance of taxation; for some of the dutied commodities were necessaries, we had them not within ourselves, were prohibited from importing them from any place except Great-Britain, were therefore obliged to import them from Great-Britain, and, consequently, were obliged to pay the duties. Accordingly, news-paper publications, pamphlets, resolves, non-importation agreements, and the whole system of American opposition, were again put in motion. We obtained a partial repeal of this statute, which took off the duties from all the articles, except teas. This was the lucky moment when to have closed the dispute. We might have made a safe and honorable retreat. We had gained much, perhaps more than we expected. If the parliament had passed an act, declaratory of their right to tax us; our assemblies had resolved, ten times, that they had no such right. We could not complain of the three-penny duty on tea as burdensome, for a shilling which had been laid upon it, for the purpose of regulating trade and therefore was allowed to be constitutional, was taken off; so that we were in fact gainers nine-pence in a pound by the new regulation. If the appropriation of the revenue, arising from this statute was disrelished, it was only our striking off one article of luxury from our manner of living, an article too, which if we may believe the resolves of most of the towns in this province, or rely on its *collected wisdom* in a resolve of the house of representatives, was to the last degree ruinous to health. It was futile to urge its being a precedent, as a reason for keeping up the ball of contention; for, allowing the supreme legislature ever to want a precedent, they had many for laying duties on commodities imported into the colonies. And besides, we had great reason to believe that the remaining part of the statute would be repealed, as soon as the parliament should suppose it could be done with honour to themselves; as the incidental revenue, arising from the former regulation, was four fold to the revenue arising from the latter. A claim of the right, could work no injury, so long as there was no grievous exercise of it;

especially

especially as we had protested against it, through the whole, and could not be said to have departed from our claims in the least. We might now upon good terms have dropped the dispute, and been happy in the affections of our mother-country; but *that* is yet to come. Party is inseparable from a free state. The several distributions of power, as they are limited by, so they create perpetual dissentions between, each other, about their respective boundaries; but the greatest source is the competition of individuals for preferment in the state. Popularity is the ladder by which the partizans usually climb.—Accordingly the struggle is, who shall have the greatest share of it. Each party professes *disinterested patriotism*, though some cynical writers have ventured to assert, that self-love is the ruling passion of the whole. There were two parties in this province of pretty long standing, known by the name of *whig* and *tory*, which at this time were not a little imbittered against each other.—Men of abilities and acknowledged probity were on both sides. If the tories were suspected of pursuing their private interest through the medium of court favour, there was equal reason to suspect the whigs of pursuing their private interest by the means of popularity. Indeed some of them owed all their importance to it, and must in a little time have sunk into obscurity, had these turbulent commotions then subsided.

The tories and whigs took different routs, as usual. The tories were for closing the controversy with Great-Britain, the whigs for continuing it : the tories were for restoring government in the province, which had become greatly relaxed by these convulsions, to its former tone; the whigs were averse to it : they even refused to revive a temporary riot act, which expired about this time. Perhaps they thought, that mobs were a necessary ingredient in their system of opposition : However, the whigs had great advantages in the unequal combat, their scheme flattered the people with the idea of independence; the tories' plan supposed a degree of subordination, which is rather an humiliating idea; besides there is a propensity in men to believe themselves injured and oppressed whenever they are told

so,

fo. The ferment, raifed in their minds in the time of the ftamp-act, was not yet allayed, and the leaders of the whigs had gained the confidence of the people by their fucceffes in their former ftruggle; fo that they had nothing to do but to keep up the fpirit among the people, and they were fure of commanding in this province. It required fome pains to prevent their minds fettling into that calm, which is or-dinarily the effect of a mild government ; the whigs were fenfible that there was no oppreffion that could be either feen or felt; if any thing was in reality amifs in govern-ment, it was its being too lax : So far was it from the in-nocent being in danger of fuffering, that the moft atrocious offenders efcaped with impunity. They accordingly ap-plied themfelves to work upon the imagination, and to inflame the paffion ; for this work they poffeffed great talents. I will do juftice to their ingenuity : they were in-timately acquainted with the feelings of man, and knew all the avenues to the human heart :—Effigies, paintings, and other imagery, were exhibited ; the fourteenth of Au-guft was celebrated annually as a feftival in commemoration of a mob's deftroying a building, owned by the late Lieu-tenant Governor, which was fuppofed to have been erected for a ftamp-office, and compelling him to refign his office of ftamp-mafter under liberty-tree ; annual orations were delivered in the old-fouth meeting houfe, on the fifth of March, the day when fome perfons were unfortunately killed by a party of the twenty-ninth regiment; lifts of imaginary grievances were continually publifhed; the people were told weekly, that the miniftry had formed a plan to enflave them ; that the duty upon tea was only a prelude to a window-tax, hearth-tax, land-tax, and poll-tax, and thefe were only paving the way for reducing the country to lordfhips : this laft bait was the more eafily fwallowed, as there feems to be an apprehenfion of that kind hereditary to the people of New-England ; and they were conjured by the duty they owed themfelves, their country, and their GOD, by the reverence due to the facred memory of their anceftors, and all their toils and fufferings in this once inhofpitable wildernefs, and by their affections for

unborn

unborn millions, to roufe and exert themfelves in the common caufe. This perpetual incantation kept the people in continual alarm. We were farther ftimulated by being told, that the people of England were depraved, the parliament venal, and the miniftry corrupt; nor were attempts wanting to traduce Majefty itfelf. The kingdom of Great-Britain was depicted as an ancient ftructure, once the admiration of the world, now fliding from its bafe, and rufhing to its fall. At the fame time, we were called upon to mark our own rapid growth, and to behold the certain evidence that America was upon the eve of independent empire.

When we confider what effect a well wrote tragedy or novel has on the human paffions, though we know it to be all fictitious; what effect muft all this be fuppofed to have had upon thofe, that believed thefe high wrought images to be realities?

The tories have been cenfured for remiffnefs in not having exerted themfelves fufficiently at this period: The truth of the cafe is this; they faw and fhuddered at the gathering ftorm, but durft not attempt to difpel it, left it fhould burft on their own heads. Printers were threatned with the lofs of their bread, for publifhing freely on the tory fide. One Mr. Mien was forced to fly the country for perfifting in it.

All our diffenting minifters were not inactive on this occafion. When the clergy engage in a political warfare, religion becomes a moft powerful engine, either to fupport or overthrow the ftate. What effect muft it have had upon the audience to hear the fame fentiments and principles which they had before read in a news-paper, delivered on Sundays from the pulpits, with a religious awe, and the moft folemn appeals to heaven, from lips which they had been taught, from their cradles, to believe could utter nothing but eternal truths? What was it natural to expect from a people, bred under a free conftitution, jealous of their liberty, credulous even to a proverb, when told their privileges were in danger, thus wrought upon in the extreme? I anfwer:—Outrages, difgraceful to humanity itfelf.

What

What mifchief was not an artful man, who had obtained the confidence and guidance of fuch an enraged multitude, capable of doing? He had only to point out this or the other man as an enemy to his country, and no character, ftation, age or merit, could protect the profcribed from their fury. Happy was it for him, if he could fecrete his perfon, and fubject his property only to their lawlefs ravages. By fuch means, many people naturally brave and humane, have been wrought upon to commit fuch acts of private mifchief and public violence, as will blacken many a page in the hiftory of our country.

I fhall next trace the effects of this fpirit, which the whigs had thus infufed into the body of the people, through the courts of common law, and the general-affembly; and mark the ways and means whereby they availed themfelves of it to the fubverfion of our charter conftitution, antecedent to the late act of parliament.

MASSACHUSETTENSIS.

December 19, 1774.

<hr>

L E T T E R   III.

To the Inhabitants of the Province of Maffachufetts-Bay.

TO undertake to convince a perfon of his error is the indifpenfable duty, the certain, though dangerous, teft of friendfhip. He that could fee his friend perfevering in a fatal error, without reminding him of it, and ftriving to reclaim him, through fear that he might thereby incur his difpleafure, would little deferve the facred name himfelf. Such delicacy is not only falfe, but criminal. Were I not fully convinced, upon the moft mature deliberation that I am capable of, that the temporal falvation of this province depends upon an entire and fpeedy change of meafures, which muft depend upon a change of fentiment, refpecting our own conduct, and the juftice of the Britifh nation; I never fhould have obtruded myfelf on the public.—I repeat my promife, to avoid perfonal reflection as much as the nature of the tafk will admit of; but I will continue faithfully to expofe the wretched policy of the whigs, tho' I may be obliged to penetrate the *arcana*, and difcover fuch

things

things as, were there not a neceffity for it, I fhould be infinitely happier in drawing a veil over, or covering with a mantle. Should I be fo unfortunate as to incur your difpleafure, I fhall neverthelefs think myfelf happy if I can but fnatch one of my fellow-fubjects as a brand out of the burning.

Perhaps fome may imagine, that I have reprefented too many of my countrymen, as well as the leading whigs, in an unjuft point of light, by fuppofing *thefe* fo wicked as to miflead, or *thofe* fo little circumfpect as to be mifled, in matters of the laft importance. Whoever has been converfant with the hiftory of man, muft know that it abounds with fuch inftances. The fame game, and with the fame fuccefs, has been played in all ages and in all countries.

The bulk of the people are generally but little verfed in matters of ftate. Want of inclination or opportunity to figure in public life, makes them content to reft the affairs of government in the hands, where accident or merit has placed them. Their views and employments are confined to the humbler walks of bufinefs or retirement. There is a latent fpark however in their breafts, capable of being kindled into a flame; to do this has always been the employment of the difaffected. They begin by reminding the people of the elevated rank they hold in the univerfe, as men; that all men by nature are equal; that Kings are but the minifters of the people; that their authority is delegated to them by the people for their good; and that they have a right to refume it, and place it in other hands, or keep it themfelves, whenever it is made ufe of to opprefs them. Doubtlefs there have been inftances, where thefe principles have been inculcated to obtain a redrefs of real grievances, but they have been much oftener perverted to the worft of purpofes.—No government, however perfect in theory, is adminiftered in perfection; the frailty of man does not admit of it. A fmall miftake, in point of policy, often furnifhes a pretence to libel government, and perfuade the people, that their rulers are tyrants, and the whole government a fyftem of oppreffion. Thus the feeds of fedition are ufually fown; and the people are led to facrifice

real

real liberty to licentioufnefs, which gradually ripens into rebellion and civil war. And what is ftill more to be lamented, the generality of the people, who are thus made the dupes of artifice, and the mere ftilts of ambition, are fure to be lofers in the end. The beft they can expect, is to be thrown neglected by, when they are no longer wanted; but they are feldom fo happy: if they are fubdued, confifcation of eftate and ignominious death are their portion; if they conquer, their own army is often turned upon them, to fubjugate them to a more tyrannical government than that they rebelled againft. Hiftory is replete with inftances of this kind: we can trace them in remote antiquity; we find them in modern times, and have a remarkable one in the very country from which we are derived. It is an univerfal truth, that he that would excite a rebellion, whatever profeffions of philanthropy he may make, when he is infinuating and worming himfelf into the good graces of the people, is at heart as great a tyrant as ever weilded the iron rod of oppreffion. I fhall have occafion hereafter to confider this matter more fully, when I fhall endeavour to convince you, how little we can gain, and how much we may lofe, by this unequal, unnatural, and defperate conteft. My prefent bufinefs is, to trace the fpirit of oppofition to Great-Britain through the general court, and the courts of common law. In moderate times, a reprefentative that votes for an unpopular meafure, or oppofes a popular one, is in danger of lofing his election the next year; when party runs high, he is fure to do it. It was the policy of the whigs to have their queftions, upon high matters, determined by yea and nay votes, which were publifhed with the reprefentatives names in the next gazette. This was commonly followed by fevere ftrictures and the moft illiberal invectives upon the diffentients: fometimes they were held up as objects of refentment, or contempt at others; the abufe was in proportion to the extravagance of the meafure they oppofed. This may feem not worth notice, but its confequences were important. The fcurrility made its way into the diffentient's town, it furnifhed his competitor with means to fupplant him,

D

him, and he took care to fhun the rock his predeceffor had fplit upon. In this temper of the times, it was enough to know who voted with Caffius and who with Lucius, to determine who was a friend and who an enemy to the country, without once adverting to the queftion before the houfe. The lofs of a feat in the houfe was not of fo much confequence; but, when once he became ftigmatized as an enemy to his country, he was expofed to infult; and if his profeffion or bufinefs was fuch, that his livelihood depended much on the good graces of his fellow citizens, he was in danger of lofing his bread and involving his whole family in ruin.

One particular fet of members, in committee, always prepared the refolves and other fpirited meafures. At firft they were canvaffed freely, at length would flide through the houfe without meeting an obftacle: The lips of the diffentients were fealed up; they fat in filence, and beheld with infinite regret the meafures they durft not oppofe. Many were borne down againft their wills by the violence of the current: upon no other principle can we reconcile their oftenfible conduct in the houfe to their declarations in private circles. The apparent unanimity in the houfe encouraged the oppofition out of doors, and *that* in its turn ftrengthened the party in the houfe. Thus they went on, mutually fupporting and up-lifting each other. Affemblies and towns refolved alternately: fome of them only omitted refolving to fnatch the fceptre out of the hands of our Sovereign, and to ftrike the imperial crown from his facred head.

A mafter-ftroke in politics, refpecting the agent, ought not to be neglected. Each colony has ufually an agent refiding at the court of Great-Britain: Thefe agents are appointed by the three branches of their feveral affemblies, and indeed there cannot be a provincial agent without fuch appointment. The whigs foon found, that they could not have fuch fervices rendered them from a provincial agent, as would anfwer their purpofes. The houfe therefore refufed to join with the other two branches of the general court in the appointment. The houfe chofe an agent for them-

themfelves; and the council appointed another. Thus we had two agents for private purpofes, and the expence of agency doubled; and with equal reafon a third might have been added, as agent for the Governor, and the charges been trebled.

The additional expence was of little confideration, compared with another inconvenience that attended this new mode of agency. The perfon, appointed by the houfe, was the oftenfible agent of the province, though in fact he was only the agent of a few individuals that had got the art of managing the houfe at their pleafure. He knew his continuing in office depended upon *them*. An office that yielded feveral hundred pounds fterling annually, the bufinefs of which confifted in little more than attending the levees of the Great, and writing letters to America, was worth preferving. Thus he was under a ftrong temptation to facrifice the province to a party; and echoed back the fentiments of his patrons.

The advices, continually received from one of the perfons that was thus appointed agent, had great influence upon the members of the houfe of more moderate principles. He had pufhed his refearches deep into nature, and made important difcoveries: they thought he had done the fame in politics, and did not admire him lefs as a politician than as a philofopher. His intelligence, as to the difpofition of his Majefty, the miniftry, the parliament, and the nation in general, was deemed the moft authentic. He advifed us to keep up our oppofition, to refolve and re-refolve, to cherifh a military fpirit; uniformly holding up this idea, that if we continued firm, we had nothing to fear from the government in England. He even propofed fome modes of oppofition himfelf. The fpirited meafures were always ufhered into the houfe with a letter from him. I have been fometimes almoft ready to fufpect him of being the *primum mobile*, and that, like the man behind the curtain at a puppet-fhew, he was playing off the figures here with his own fecret wires. If he advifed to thefe meafures contrary to his better knowledge, from finifter views, and to ferve a private purpofe, he has *wilfully* done the province irrepa-

D 2   rable

rable injury. However, I will do him juſtice: he enjoined it upon us to refrain from violence, as that would unite the nation againſt us; and I am rather inclined to think that he was deceived himſelf with reſpect to the meaſures he recommended, as he had already felt the reſentment of that very government which he told us there was nothing to fear from. This diſpoſition of the houſe could not have produced ſuch fatal effects, had the other two branches of the legiſlature retained their conſtitutional freedom and influence. They might have been a ſufficient check.

The councillors depended upon the general aſſembly for their political exiſtence: the whigs reminded the council of their mortality. If a councillor oppoſed the violent meaſures of the whigs with any ſpirit, he loſt his election the next May. The council conſiſted of twenty-eight. From this principle, near half that number, moſtly men of the firſt families, note and abilities, with every poſſible attachment to their native country, and as far from temptation as wealth and independence could remove them, were tumbled from their ſeats in diſgrace. Thus the board, which was intended to moderate between the two extremes of prerogative and privilege, loſt its weight in the ſcale, and the political balance of the province was deſtroyed.

Had the chair been able to retain its own conſtitutional influence, the loſs of the board would have been leſs felt; but, no longer ſupported by the board, that fell likewiſe. The Governor, by the charter, could do little or nothing without the council. If he called upon a military officer to raiſe the militia, he was anſwered, they were there already. If he called upon his council for their aſſiſtance, they muſt firſt enquire into the cauſe. If he wrote to government at home to ſtrengthen his hands, ſome officious perſons procured and ſent back his letters.

It was not the perſon of a Bernard or Hutchinſon that made them obnoxious: any other governors would have met with the ſame fate, had they diſcharged their duty with equal fidelity; that is, had they ſtrenuouſly oppoſed the principles and practices of the whigs; and when they found that the government here could not ſupport itſelf,

wrote

wrote home for aid fufficient to do it. And let me tell you, had the intimations in thofe letters, which you are taught to execrate, been timely attended to, we had been as happy a people as good government could make us. Governor Bernard came here recommended by the affections of the province, over which he had prefided. His abilities are acknowledged. True Britifh honefty and punctuality are traits in his character too ftrongly marked to efcape the eye of prejudice itfelf. We know Governor Hutchinfon to be amiable and exemplary in private life : his great abilities, integrity and humanity, were confpicuous in the feveral important departments that he filled, before his appointment to the chair, and reflect honour on his native country. But his abilities and integrity, added to his thorough knowledge of the province, in all its interefts and connections, were infufficient in this cafe. The conftitution itfelf was gone, though the ancient form remained : the fpirit was truly republican. He endeavoured to reclaim us by gentle means. He ftrove to convince us by arguments, drawn from the firft principles of government, our feveral charters, and the exprefs acknowledgments of our anceftors, that our claims were inconfiftent with the fubordination due to Great-Britain ; and, if perfifted in, might work the deftruction of thofe that we were entitled to. For this, he was called an enemy to his country, and fet up as a mark for the envenomed arrows of malice and party rage. Had I entertained a doubt about its being the governor, and not the man, that was aimed at ; the admirable facility with which the news-paper abufe was transferred from Governor Hutchinfon to his humane and benevolent fucceffor, General Gage, almoft as foon as he fet foot on our fhore, would have removed it.

Thus, difaffection to Great-Britain being infufed into the body of the people, the fubtle poifon ftole through all the veins and arteries, contaminated the blood, and deftroyed the very ftamina of the conftitution. Had not the courts of juftice been tainted in the early ftages, our government might have expelled the virus, purged off the peccant humors, and recovered its former vigour by its own ftrength.
The

The judges of the superior courts were dependent upon the annual grants of the general court for their support. Their salaries were small in proportion to the salaries of other officers in the government of less importance.

They had often petitioned the assembly to enlarge them, without success. They were at this time reminded of their dependence. However, it is but justice to say, that the judges remained unshaken, amid the raging tempests, which is to be attributed rather to their firmness than situation. But the spirit of the times was very apparent in the juries. The grand jurors were elective; and in such places where libels, riots, and infurrections were the most frequent, the high whigs took care to get themselves chosen. The judges pointed out to them the feditious libels on governors, magistrates, and the whole government; but to no effect. They were enjoined to present riots and infurrections, of which there was ample evidence, with as little success.

It is difficult to account for so many of the first rate whigs being returned to serve on the petit-jury at the term next after extraordinary infurrections, without suppofing some legerdemain in drawing their names out of the box. It is certain, that, notwithstanding swarms of the most virulent libels infested the province, and there were so many riots and infurrections, scarce one offender was indicted, and I think not one convicted and punished. Causes of *meum et tuum* were not always exempt from party influence. The mere circumstance of the whigs gaining the afcendency over the tories is trifling. Had the whigs divided the province between them, as they once flattered themselves they should be able to do, it would have been of little consequence to the community, had they not cut afunder the very finews of government, and broke in pieces the ligaments of focial life in the attempt. I will mention two instances, which I have selected out of many, of the weakness of our government, as they are recent and unconnected with acts of parliament. One Malcolm, a loyal subject, and, as such, entitled to protection, the evening before the last winter feffions of the general-court, was dragged out of his house, stripped, tarred and feathered,

and

and carted feveral hours in the fevereft froft of that winter, to the utmoft hazard of his life. He was carried to the gallows with an halter about his neck, and, in his paffage to and from the gallows, was beaten with as cruel ftripes as ever were adminiftered by the hands of a favage. The whipping, however, kept up the circulation of his blood, and faved the poor man's life. When they had fatiated their malice, they difperfed in good order. This was tranf-acted in the prefence of thoufands of fpectators, fome of whom were members of the general-court. Malcolm's life was defpaired of feveral days, but he furvived and pre-fented a memorial to the general-affembly, praying their in-terpofition. The petition was read, and all he obtained was, leave to withdraw it. So that he was deftitute of pro-tection every hour until he left the country; as were thou-fands befide, until the arrival of the King's troops. This originated in a fmall fracas in the ftreet, wherein Malcolm ftruck, or threatened to ftrike, a perfon that infulted him, with a cutlafs, and had no connection with the quarrel of the times, unlefs his fuftaining a fmall poft in the cuftoms made it.

The other inftance is much ftronger than this, as it was totally detached from politics. It had been fufpected, that infection had been communicated from an hofpital, lately erected at Marblehead, for the purpofe of innocula-ting the fmall-pox, to the town's people. This caufed a great infurrection: the infurgents burnt the hofpital; not content with that, threatened the proprietors and many others, fome of the firft fortunes and characters in the town, with burning their houfes over their heads, and continued parading the ftreets, to the utmoft terror of the inhabitants feveral days. A maffacre and general devafta-tion was apprehended. The perfons threatened, armed them-felves, and petitioned the general-affembly, which was then fitting, for affiftance, as there was little or no civil authority in the place. A committee was ordered to re-pair to Marblehead, report the facts, and inquire into the caufe. The committee reported the facts nearly as ftated in the petition; the report was accepted, and nothing far-ther done by the affembly. Such demonftrations of the

weak-

weaknefs of government, induced many perfons to join the whigs, to feek from them that protection, which the conftitutional authority of the province was unable to afford.

Government, at home, early in the day, made an effort to check us in our career, and to enable us to recover from anarchy without her being driven to the neceffity of altering our provincial conftitution, knowing the predilection that people always have for an antient form of government. The judges of the fuperior court had not been ftaggered, though their feet ftood in flippery places ; they depended upon the leading whigs for their fupport. To keep them fteady, they were made independent of the grants of the general-affembly. But it was not a remedy any way adequate to the difeafe. The whigs now turned their artillery againft them ; and it played brifkly.—The chief juftice, for accepting the crown grant, was accufed of receiving a royal bribe.

Thus, my friends, thofe very perfons, who had made you believe, that every attempt to ftrengthen government, and fave our charter, was an infringement of your privileges ; by little and little, deftroyed your real liberty, fubverted your charter conftitution, abridged the freedom of the houfe, annihilated the freedom of the board, and rendered the governor a mere doge of Venice. They engroffed all the power of the province into their own hands : A democracy or republic it has been called, but it does not deferve the name of either—It was, however, a defpotifm, cruelly carried into execution by mobs and riots, and more incompatible with the rights of mankind, than the enormous monarchies of the Eaft. The abfolute neceffity of the interpofition of parliament is apparent. The good policy of the act, for regulating the government in this province, will be the fubject of fome future paper. A particular Inquiry into the defpotifm of the whigs will be deferred for a chapter on congreffes. I fhall next afk your attention to a tranfaction, as important in its confequences, and perhaps more fo, than any I have yet mentioned, I mean the deftruction of the tea, belonging to the Eaft-India company. I am fenfible of the difficulty of the tafk, in combating generally

nerally received opinions. It is hard work to eradicate
deep-rooted prejudice. But I will perfevere. There are
hundreds, if not thoufands, in the province, that will feel
the truth of what I have written, line by line, as they read it;
and as to thofe who obftinately fhut their eyes againft it now,
haply the fever of the times may intermit; there may be
fome lucid interval when their minds fhall be open to truth
before it is too late to ferve them, otherwife it will be re-
vealed to them in bitter moments, attended with keen re-
morfe and unutterable anguifh. *Magna eft veritas et præ-
valebit.*

MASSACHUSETTENSIS.

December 26, 1774.

L E T T E R   III.

To the Inhabitants of the Province of Maffachufetts-Bay.

PERHAPS, by this time, fome of you may enquire who
it is, that fuffers his pen to run fo freely? I will tell
you; it is a native of this province, that knew it before
many, that are now bafking in the rays of political funfhine,
had a being. He was favored, not by whigs or tories, but
the people, with fuch a ftand in the community, as that he
could diftinctly fee all the political manœuvres of the province. He faw fome with pleafure, others with pain. If
he condemns the conduct of the whigs, he does not always
approve of the conduct of the tories. He dwells upon
the mifconduct of the former, becaufe we are indebted to
that for bringing us into this wretched ftate; unlefs the fu-
pinenefs of the latter, at fome periods, and fome impolitic
efforts to check the whigs in their career, at others, that
ferved like adding fuel to the fire, ought to be added to the
account. He is now repaying your favours, if he knows
his own heart, from the pureft gratitude and the moft un-
diffembled patriotifm, which will one day be acknowledged.
I faw the fmall feed of fedition, when it was implanted: it
was, as a grain of muftard. I have watched the plant until it has become a great tree; the vileft reptiles that crawl
upon the earth, are concealed at the root; the fouleft birds
E of

of the air reft upon its branches. I now would induce you
to go to work immediately with axes and hatchets, and
cut it down, for a two-fold reafon; becaufe it is a peft to
fociety, and left it be felled fuddenly by a ftronger arm,
and crufh its thoufands in the fall.

An apprehenfion of injuftice in the conduct of Great-
Britain towards us, I have already told you was one fource
of our mifery. Laft week I endeavoured to convince you
of the neceffity of her regulating, or rather eftablifhing,
fome government amongft us. I am now to point out the
principles and motives, upon which the blockade act was
made. The violent attack upon the property of the Eaft-
India company, in the deftruction of their tea, was the
caufe of it. In order to form a right judgment of that
tranfaction, it is neceffary to go back and view the caufe
of its being fent here. As the government of England is
mixt, fo the fpirit or genius of the nation is at once monarchical, ariftocratical, democratical, martial, and commercial. It is difficult to determine, which is the moft predominant principle; but it is worthy of remark, that to injure
the Britifh nation upon either of thefe points, is like in-
juring a Frenchman in the point of honor. Commerce is
the great fource of national wealth; for this reafon it is
cherifhed by all orders of men from the palace to the cot-
tage. In fome countries, a merchant is held in contempt
by the nobles; in England they refpect him. He rifes to
high honors in the ftate, often contracts alliances with the
firft families in the kingdom, and noble blood flows in the
veins of his pofterity. Trade is founded upon perfons or
countries mutually fupplying each other with their redun-
dances. Thus none are impoverifhed, all enriched, the
afperities of human life worn away, and mankind made
happier by it. Hufbandry, manufacture, and merchandize
are its triple fupport: deprived of either of thefe, it would
ceafe.

Agriculture is the natural livelihood of a country but
thinly inhabited, as arts and manufactures are of a popu-
lous one. The high price of labour prevents manufactures
being carried on to advantage in the firft; fcarcity of foil
obliges

obliges the inhabitants to purfue them in the latter. Upon thefe, and the confiderations arifing from the fertility and produce of different climates, and fuch like principles, the grand fyftem of the Britifh trade is founded. The collected wifdom of the nation has always been attentive to this great point of policy, that the national trade might be fo balanced and poifed, as that each part of her extended dominions might be benefited, and the whole concentre to the good of the empire. This evinces the neceffity of acts for regulating trade.

To prevent one part of the empire being enriched at the expence and to the impoverifhing of another, checks, reftrictions, and fometimes abfolute prohibitions, are neceffary. Thefe are impofed or taken off as circumftances vary. To carry the acts of trade into execution, many officers are neceffary. Thus we fee a number of cuftom-houfe officers fo conftituted, as to be checks and controuls upon each other, and prevent their fwerving from their duty, fhould they be tempted; and a board of commiffioners appointed to fuperintend the whole, like the commiffioners of the cuftoms in England. Hence alfo arifes the neceffity of courts of admiralty.

The laws and regulations of trade are efteemed in England as facred. An eftate made by fmuggling, or purfuing an illicit trade, is there looked upon as filthy lucre, as monies amaffed by gaming; and upon the fame principle, becaufe it is obtained at the expence and often ruin of others. The fmuggler not only injures the public, but often ruins the fair trader.

The great extent of fea-coaft, many harbours, the variety of iflands, the numerous creeks and navigable rivers, afford the greateft opportunity to drive an illicit trade in thefe colonies without detection. This advantage has not been overlooked by the avaricious, and many perfons feem to have fet the laws of trade at a defiance. This accounts for fo many new regulations being made, new officers appointed, and fhips of war from time to time ftationed along the continent. The way to *Holland* and back again is well known; and by much the greateft part of the tea that has

E 2   been

been drank in America for several years, has been imported from thence and other places, in direct violation of law. By this the smugglers have amassed great estates, to the prejudice of the fair trader. It was sensibly felt by the East-India company; they were prohibited from exporting their teas to America, and were obliged to sell it at auction in London; the London merchant purchased it, and put a profit upon it when he shipt it for America; the American merchant, in his turn, put a profit upon it, and after him the shopkeeper; so that it came to the consumers hands, at a very advanced price. Such quantities of tea were annually smuggled, that it was scarcely worth while for the American merchant to import tea from England at all. Some of the principal trading towns in America were wholly supplied with this commodity by smuggling: Boston however continued to import it, until advice was received that the parliament had it in contemplation to permit the East-India company to send their teas directly to America. The Boston merchants then sent their orders conditionally to their correspondents in England, to have tea shipt for them, in case the East-India company's tea did not come out. One merchant, a great whig, had such an order lying in England for sixty chests, on his own account, when the company's tea was sent. An act of parliament was made to enable the East-India company to send their tea directly to America, and sell it at auction there; not with a view of raising a revenue from the three-penny duty, but to put it out of the power of the smugglers to injure them by their infamous trade. We have it from good authority, that the revenue was not the consideration before parliament; and it is reasonable to suppose it: for had *that* been the point in view, it was only to restore the former regulation, which was then allowed to be constitutional, and the revenue would have been respectable. Had this new regulation taken effect, the people in America would have been great gainers. The wholesale merchant might have been deprived of some of his gains; but the retailer would have supplied himself with this article, directly from the auction, and the consumer reap the benefit; as tea would have been

sold

fold, under the price that had been ufual, by near one half.
Thus the country in general would have been great gainers, the Eaft-India company fecured in fupplying the A-
merican markets with this article, which they are entitled
to by the laws of trade, and fmuggling fuppreffed, at leaft
as to tea. A fmuggler and a whig are coufin-germans,
the offspring of two fifters, avarice and ambition. They
had been playing into each others hands a long time. The
fmuggler received protection from the whig ; and he, in his
turn, received fupport from the fmuggler. The illicit trader
now demanded protection from his kinfman, and it would
have been unnatural in him to have refufed it ; and befide,
an opportunity prefented of ftrengthening his own intereft.
The confignees were connected with the tories, and that
was a further ftimulus.—Accordingly, the prefs was.again
fet to work, and the old ftory repeated with additions about
monopolies ; and many infatuated perfons once more
wrought up to a proper pitch to carry into execution any
violent meafures, that their leaders fhould propofe. A bold
ftroke was refolved upon. The whigs, though they had
got the art of managing the people, had too much fenfe to
be ignorant that it was all a meer fineffe, not only without,
but directly repugnant to law, conftitution and government,
and could not laft always. They determined to put all at
hazard, and to be *aut Cæfar aut nihil.* The approaching
ftorm was forefeen ; and the firft fhip that arrived with the
tea was detained below Caftle-William. A body meeting was
affembled at the old-fouth meeting-houfe, which has great
advantage over a town-meeting, as no law has yet afcer-
tained the qualification of the voters ; each perfon prefent,
of whatever age, eftate, or country, may take the liberty to
fpeak or vote at fuch an affembly; and that may ferve as
a fkreen to the town where it originated, in cafe of any
difaftrous confequence. The body-meeting confifting of
feveral thoufands, being thus affembled, with the leading
whigs at its head, in the firft place fent for the owner of
the tea-fhip, and required him to bring her to the wharf,
upon pain of their difpleafure ; the fhip was accordingly
brought up, and the mafter was obliged to enter at the
cuftom-

cuftom-houfe: He reported the tea, after which twenty days are allowed for landing it and paying the duty.

The next ftep was to refolve.—They refolved that the tea fhould not be landed, nor the duty paid, that it fhould go home in the fame bottom that it came in, &c. &c. This was the fame as refolving to deftroy it, for as the fhip had been compelled to come to the wharf, and was entered at the cuftom-houfe, it could not, by law, be cleared out, without the duties being firft paid, nor could the Governor grant a permit for the veffel to pafs Caftle-William, without a certificate from the cuftom-houfe of fuch clearance, confiftent with his duty. The body accordingly ordered a military guard to watch the fhip every night untii further orders. The confignees had been applied to, by the felectmen, to fend the tea to England: they anfwered, they could not, for if they did, it would be forfeited by the acts of trade, and they fhould be liable to make good the lofs to the Eaft-India company. Some of the confignees were mobbed, and all were obliged to fly to the caftle, and there immure themfelves. They petitioned the Governor and Council to take the property of the Eaft-India company under their protection. The council declined being concerned in it. The confignees then offered the body to ftore the tea under the care of the felectmen or a committee of the town of Bofton, and to have no further concern in the matter until they could fend to England, and receive further inftructions from their principals. This was refufed with difdain. The military guard was regularly kept in rotation till the eve of the twentieth day, when the duties muft have been paid, the tea landed, or be liable to feizure; then the military guard was withdrawn, or rather omitted being pofted; and a number of perfons in difguife forceably entered the fhips (three being by this time arrived) fplit open the chefts, and emptied all the tea, being of ten thoufand pounds fterling value, into the dock, and perfumed the town with its fragrance. Another circumftance ought not to be omitted: the afternoon before the deftruction of the tea, the body fent the owner of one of the fhips to the Governor, to demand a pafs; he anfwered, that he

would

would as soon give a pass for that as any other vessel, if he had the proper certificate from the custom-house, without which he could not give a pass for any, consistent with his duty. It was known that this would be the answer, when the message was sent; and it was with the utmost difficulty that the body were kept together till the messenger returned. When the report was made, a shout was set up in the galleries and at the door, and the meeting immediately dispersed. The Governor had, previous to this, sent a proclamation by the sheriff, commanding the body to disperse; they permitted it to be read, and answered it with a general hiss. These are the facts as truly and fairly stated, as I am able to state them. The ostensible reason for this conduct, was the tea's being subject to the three-penny duty. Let us take the advocates for this transaction upon their own principle, and admit the duty to be unconstitutional, and see how the argument stands. Here is a cargo of tea, subject, upon its being entered and landed, to a duty of three-pence per pound, which is paid by the East-India company, or by their factors, which amounts to the same thing. Unless we purchase the tea, we shall never pay the duty; if we purchase it, we pay the three-pence included in the price; therefore, lest we should purchase it, we have a right to destroy it A flimsy pretext! and it either supposes the people destitute of virtue, or that their purchasing of the tea was a matter of no importance to the community; but even this gauze covering is stripped off, when we consider, that the Boston merchants, and some who were active at the body-meeting, were every day importing from England large quantities of tea, subject to the same duty, and vending it unmolested; and at this time had orders lying in their correspondents hands, to send them considerable quantities of tea, in case the East-India company should not send it themselves.

When the news of this transaction arrived in England, and it was considered in what manner almost every other regulation of trade had been evaded by artifice, and when artifice could no longer serve, recourse was had to violence;
the

the Britifh lion was roufed. The crown-lawyers were called upon for the law; they anfwered, high-treafon. Had
a Cromwell, whom fome amongft us deify and imitate, in
all his imitable perfections, had the guidance of the national ire ; unlefs compenfation had been made to the fufferers immediately upon its being demanded, your proud
capital had been levelled with the duft ; not content with
that, rivers of blood would have been fhed to make atone-
ment for the injured honour of the nation. It was debated
whether to attaint the principals of treafon. We have a
gracious king upon the throne, he felt the refentment of a
man, foftened by the relentings of a parent. The bowels
of our mother country yearned towards her refractory, ob-
ftinate child.

It was determined to confider the offence in a milder
light, and to compel an indemnification for the fufferers,
and prevent the like for the future, by fuch means as would
be mild, compared with the infult to the nation, or fevere,
as our future conduct fhould be : That was to depend upon
us. Accordingly, the blockade act was paffed ; and had
an act of juftice been done in indemnifying the fufferers,
and an act of loyalty in putting a ftop to feditious practices, our port had long fince been opened. This act has
been called unjuft, becaufe it involves the innocent in the
fame predicament with the guilty : But it ought to be confidered, that our news-papers had announced to the world,
that feveral thoufands attended thofe body-meetings ; and
it did not appear, that there was one diffentient, or any
proteft entered. I do not know, how a perfon could expect diftinction in fuch a cafe, if he neglected to diftinguifh himfelf. When the noble lord propofed it in the
houfe of commons, he called upon all the members prefent to mention a better method of obtaining juftice in this
cafe: fcarce one denied the neceffity of doing fomething ;
but none could mention a more eligible way. Even minifterial oppofition was abafhed. If any parts of the act
ftrike us, like the feverity of a mafter ; let us coolly advert to the aggravated infult, and, perhaps, we fhall wonder at the lenity of a parent. After this tranfaction, all
parties

parties feem to have laid upon their oars, waiting to fee
what parliament would do. When the blockade act arrived, many and many were defirous of paying for the tea
immediately; and fome, who were guiltlefs of the crime,
offered to contribute to the compenfation : but our leading
whigs muft ftill rule the roaft, and that inaufpicious influence, that had led us hitherto, plunged us ftill deeper
in mifery. The whigs faw their ruin connected with a compliance with the terms of opening the port; as it would
afford a convincing proof of the wretchednefs of their policy in the deftruction of the tea, and as they might juftly
have been expected to pay the money demanded themfelves;
and fo fet themfelves induftrioufly to work to prevent it,
and engage the other colonies to efpoufe their caufe.

This was a crifis too important and alarming to the province to be neglected by its friends. A number of as refpectable perfons as any in this province, belonging to
Bofton, Cambridge, Salem, and Marblehead, now came
forward, publicly to difavow the proceedings of the whigs,
to do juftice to the much injured character of Mr. Hutchinfon, and to ftrengthen his influence at the court of Great-
Britain, where he was going to receive the well-deferved
plaudit of his fovereign, that he might be able to obtain a
repeal or fome mitigation of that act, the terms of which,
they forefaw, the perverfenefs of the whigs would prevent
a compliance with. This was done by feveral addreffes,
which were fubfcribed by upwards of two hundred perfons,
and would have been by many more, had not the fudden
embarkation of Mr. Hutchinfon prevented it. The juftices
of the court of common pleas and general feffions of the
peace, for the county of Plymouth, fent their addrefs to him
in England. There were fome of almoft all orders of men,
among thefe addreffers; but they confifted principally of men
of property, and of large family connections; and feveral were
independent in their circumftances, and lived wholly upon
the income of their eftates. Some indeed might be called
partizans; but a very confiderable proportion were perfons
that had, of choice, kept themfelves at a diftance from the
political vortex, had beheld the competition of the whigs

F   and

and tories, without any emotion; while the community remained fafe, had looked down on the political dance, in
its various mazes and intricacies, and faw one falling, another rifing, rather as a matter of amufement: but, when
they faw the capital of the province upon the point of being facrificed by political cunning, it called up all their
feelings.

Their motives were truly patriotic. Let us now attend
to the ways and means by which the whigs prevented thefe
exertions producing a good effect. Previous to this, a new
and, till lately unheard of, mode of oppofition had been
devifed, faid to be the invention of the fertile brain of one
of our party agents, called a committee of correfpondence.
This is the fouleft, fubtleft and moft venomous ferpent,
that ever iffued from the eggs of fedition. Thefe committees generally confift of the higheft whigs, or at leaft
there is fome high whig among them, that is the ruling fpirit
of the whole. They are commonly appointed at thin·
town-meetings, or if the meetings happen to be full, the
moderate men feldom fpeak or act at all when this fort of
bufinefs comes on. They have been by much too modeft.
Thus the meeting is often prefaced with " At a full town-
meeting," and the feveral refolves headed with *ncm. con.*
with ftrict truth; when, in fact, but a fmall proportion of
the town have had a hand in the matter. It is faid that
the committee for the town of Bofton was appointed for a
fpecial purpofe, and that their commiffion long fince expired. However that may be, thefe committees, when once
eftablifhed, think themfelves amenable to none; they affume
a dictatorial ftile, and have an opportunity, under the apparent fanction of their feveral towns, of clandeftinely
wreaking private revenge on individuals, by traducing
their characters, and holding them up as enemies to their
country wherever they go, as alfo of mifreprefenting facts
and propagating fedition through the country. Thus, a man
of principle and property, in travelling through the country, would be infulted by perfons whofe faces he had never
before feen, he would often feel the fmart without fufpect-
ing the hand that adminiftred the blow. Thefe committees,

tees, as they are not known in law, and can derive no authority from thence, left they fhould not get their fhare of
power, fometimes engrofs it all; they frequently erect
themfelves into a tribunal, where the fame perfons are at
once legiflator, accufers, witneffes, judges and jurors, and
the mob the executioners. The accufed has no day in
court, and the execution of the fentence is the firft notice
he receives. This is the channel through which liberty
matters have been chiefly conducted the fummer and fall
paft. This accounts for the fame diftempers breaking out
in different parts of the province at one and the fame time,
which might be attributed to fomething fupernatural by
thofe that were unacquainted with the fecret conductors of
the infection. It is chiefly owing to thefe committees, that
fo many refpectable perfons have been abufed, and forced
to fign recantations and refignations ; that fo many perfons, to avoid fuch reiterated infults, as are more to be
deprecated by a man of fentiment than death itfelf, have
been obliged to quit their houfes, families and bufinefs,
and fly to the army for protection; that hufband has been
feparated from wife, father from fon, brother from brother, the fweet intercourfe of conjugal and natural affection
interrupted, and the unfortunate refugee forced to abandon
all the comforts of domeftic life. My countrymen, I beg
you to paufe and reflect on this conduct : have not thefe
people, that are thus infulted, as good a right to think
and act for themfelves in matters of the laft importance as
the whigs ? Are they not as clofely connected with the intereft of their country as the whigs ? Do not their former
lives and converfations appear to have been regulated by
principle, as much as thofe of the whigs ? You muft anfwer, yes. Why then do you fuffer them to be cruelly treated for differing in fentiment from you ? Is it confiftent with
that liberty you profefs ? Let us wave the confideration of
right and liberty, and fee if this conduct can be reconcil-
ed to good policy. Do you expect to make converts by it?
Perfecution has the fame effect in politics, that it has in religion ; it confirms the fectary. Do you wifh to filence
them, that the inhabitants of the province may appear una-

nimous ?

nimous ? The mal-treatment they received for differing
from you, is an undeniable evidence that we are not unanimous. It may not be amifs to confider, that this is a
changeable world, and time's rolling wheel may, ere long,
bring them uppermoft ; in that cafe, I am fure you would
not wifh to have them fraught with refentment. It is afto-
nifhing, my friends, that thofe, who are in purfuit of liberty, fhould ever fuffer arbitrary power, in fuch an hideous
form and fqualid hue, to get a footing among them. I appeal to your good fenfe ; I know you have it, and hope to
penetrate to it, before I have finifhed my publications, notwithftanding the thick atmofphere that now invelopes it.
But, to return from my digreffion. The committee of
correfpondence reprefented the deftruction of the tea *in their
own way*. They reprefented thofe that addreffed Governor
Hutchinfon, as perfons of no note or property ; as mean,
bafe wretches and feekers, who had been facrificing their
country in adulation of him. Whole nations have wor-
fhipped the rifing, but, if this be an inftance, it is the only
inftance of people's worfhipping the fetting, fun. By this
means, the humane and benevolent in various parts of the
continent, were induced to advife us not to comply with the
terms for opening our port, and engaged to relieve us with
their charities, from the diftrefs that muft otherwife fall upon
the poor. Their charitable intentions may afcend to heaven, like incenfe from the altar, in fweet memorial before
the throne of God ; but their donations came near proving
fatal to the province : It encouraged the whigs to perfevere
in injuftice, and has been the means of feducing many an
honeft man into the commiffion of a crime, that he did not
fufpect himfelf capable of being guilty of. What I have
told you, are not the fuggeftions of a fpeculatift ; there are
fome miftakes as to numbers, and there may be fome as
to time and place, partly owing to mifcopying, and partly
to my not always having the books and papers neceffary
to greater accuracy, at hand ; but the relation of facts is in
fubftance true, I had almoft faid, as holy writ.—I do not
afk you to take the truths of them from an anonymous writer : The evidence of moft of them is within your reach,
examine for yourfelves :—I promife, that the benefit you
will

will reap therefrom will abundantly pay you for the trouble of the refearch; you will find, I have faithfully unriddled the whole myftery of our political iniquity. I do not addrefs myfelf to whigs or tories, but to the *whole people*. I know you well. You are loyal at heart, friends to good order, and do violence to yourfelves in harbouring, one moment, difrefpectful fentiments towards Great-Britain, the land of our forefathers' nativity, and facred repofitory of their bones: but you have been moft infidiouffly induced to believe, that Great-Britain is rapacious, cruel, and vindictive, and envies us the inheritance purchafed by the fweat and blood of our anceftors. Could that thick mift that hovers over the land, and involves it in more than Egyptian darknefs, be but once difpelled, that you might fee our fovereign the provident father of all his people, and Great-Britain a nurfing mother to thefe colonies, as they really are; long live our gracious king, and happinefs to Britain, would refound from one end of the province to the other.

MASSACHUSETTENSIS.

January 2, 1775.

L E T T E R   V.

To the Inhabitants of the Province of Maffachufetts-Bay.

My dear Countrymen.

SOME of you may perhaps fufpect that I have been wantonly fcattering firebrands, arrows and death, to gratify a malicious and revengeful difpofition: The truth is this; I had feen many excellent detached pieces, but could fee no pen at work to trace our calamity to its fource, and point out the many adventitious aids, that confpired to raife it to its prefent height; though I impatiently expected it, being fully convinced that you wait only to know the true ftate of facts, to rectify whatever is amifs in the province, without any foreign affiftance. Others may be induced to think, that I grudge the induftrious poor of Bofton their fcantlings of charity. I will iffue a brief in their favour. The opulent, be their political fentiments what they may, ought to relieve them from their fufferings,

and

and thofe who, by former donations, have been the innocent
caufe of protracting their fufferings, are under a tenfold
obligation to affift them now; and at the fame time to
make the moft explicit declarations, that they did not intend to promote nor ever will join in rebellion. Great al-
lowances are to be made for the croffings, windings and
tergiverfations of a politician : he is a cunning animal, and
as government is faid to be founded in opinion, his tricks
may be a part of the *arcana imperii*. Had our politicians
confined themfelves within any reafonable bounds, I never
fhould have molefted them ; but when I became fatisfied,
that many innocent, unfufpecting perfons were in danger
of being drenched with blood and carnage, I could reftrain
my emotions no longer; and, having once broke the bands
of natural referve, was determined to probe the fore to the
bottom, though I was fure to touch the quick. It is very
foreign from my intentions to draw down the vengeance of
Great-Britain upon the whigs ; they are too valuable a
part of the community to lofe, if they will permit themfelves to be faved: I wifh nothing worfe to the higheft of
them, than that they may be deprived of their influence,
till fuch time as they fhall have changed their fentiments,
principles and meafures.

Sedition has already been marked through its zigzag
path to the prefent times. When the ftatute for regula-
ing the government arrived, a match was put to the train,
and the mine, that had been long forming, fprung, and
threw the whole province into confufion and anarchy. The
occurrences of the fummer and autumn paft are fo recent
and notorious, that a particular detail of them is unnecef-
fary. Suffice it to fay, that every barrier that civil government had erected for the fecurity of property, liberty
and life, was broken down; and law, conftitution and government trampled under by the rudeft invaders. I fhall
not dwell upon thefe harfh notes much longer. I fhall yet
become an advocate for the leading whigs ; much muft
be allowed to men in their fituation, forcibly actuated by
the chagrin of difappointment, the fear of punifhment, and
the fafcination of hope at the fame time.

Perhaps

Perhaps the whole story of empire does not furnish another instance of a forcible opposition to government with so much specious and so little real cause, witn such apparent probability without any possibility of success. The stamp-act gave the alarm. The instability of the public counsels, from the Grenvillian administration to the appointment of the earl of Hillsborough to the American department, afforded as great a prospect of success, as the heavy duties, imposed by the stamp-act, did a colour for the opposition. It was necessary to give the history of this matter in its course, offend who it would, because those acts of government, that are called the greatest grievances, became proper and necessary, through the misconduct of our politicians; and the justice of Great-Britain towards us, could not be made apparent without first pointing out that. I intend to consider the acts of the British government, which are held up as the principal grievances, and enquire whether Great-Britain is chargeable with injustice in any one of them; but must first ask your attention to the authority of parliament. I suspect many of our politicians are wrong in their first principle, in denying that the constitutional authority of parliament extends to the colonies; if so, it must not be wondered at, that their whole fabric is so ruinous: I shall not travel through all the arguments that have been adduced, for and against this question, but attempt to reduce the substance of them to a narrow compass, after having taken a cursory view of the British constitution.

The security of the people from internal rapacity and violence, and from foreign invasion, is the end and design of government. The simple forms of government are monarchy, aristocracy and democracy, that is, where the authority of the state is vested in *one*, a *few*, or the *many*. Each of these species of government has advantages peculiar to itself, and would answer the ends of government, were the persons, intrusted with the authority of the state, always guided themselves by unerring wisdom and public virtue; but rulers are not always exempt from the weakness and depravity, which make government necessary to society.

Thus

Thus monarchy is apt to rush headlong into tyranny, ariftocracy to beget faction and multiplied ufurpation, and democracy to degenerate into tumult, violence and anarchy. A government, formed upon thefe three principles in due proportion, is the beft calculated to anfwer the ends of government, and to endure. Such a government is the Britifh conftitution, confifting of King, Lords and Commons, which at once includes the principal excellencies, and excludes the principal defects of the other kinds of government. It is allowed, both by Englifhmen and foreigners, to be the moft perfect fyftem that the wifdom of ages has produced. The diftributions of power are fo juft, and the proportions fo exact, as at once to fupport and controul each other. An Englifhman glories in being fubject to and protected by fuch a government. The colonies are a part of the Britifh empire.. The beft writers upon the laws of nations tell us, that when a nation takes poffeffion of a diftant country, and fettles there, that country, though feparated from the principal eftablifhment or mother-country, naturally becomes a part of the ftate, equal with its ancient poffeffions. Two fupreme or independent authorities cannot exift in the fame ftate. It would be what is called *imperium in imperio*, and the height of political abfurdity. The analogy between the political and human body is great. Two independent authorities in a ftate would be like two diftinct principles of volition and action in the human body, diffenting, oppofing, and deftroying each other. If then we are a part of the Britifh empire, we muft be fubject to the fupreme power of the ftate, which is vefted in the eftates of parliament, notwithftanding each of the colonies have legiflative and executive powers of their own, delegated or granted to them for the purpofes of regulating their own internal police, which are fubordinate, and muft neceffarily be fubject, to the checks, controul and regulation of the fupreme authority.

This doctrine is not new ; but the denial of it is. It is beyond a doubt that it was the fenfe both of the parent country and our anceftors, that they were to remain fubject to parliament ; it is evident from the charter itfelf, and

this

this authority has been exercifed by parliament, from time
to time, almoft ever fince the firft fettlement of the country, and has been exprefsly acknowledged by our provincial legiflatures   It is not lefs our intereft than our duty to
continue fubject to the authority of parliament, which will
be more fully confidered hereafter.   The principal argument againft the authority is this ; the Americans are entitled to all the privileges of an englifhman ; it is the privilege of an englifhman to be exempt from all laws that he
does not confent to in perfon, or by reprefentative ; the Americans are not reprefented in parliament, and therefore are exempt from acts of parliament, or, in other words, not fubject to
its authority. This appears fpecious ; but leads to fuch ab-
furdities as demonftrate its fallacy.   If the colonies are not
fubject to the authority of parliament, Great-Britain and
the colonies muft be diftinct ftates, as completely fo as
England and Scotland were before the union, or as Great-
Britain and Hanover are now.   The colonies in that cafe
will owe no allegiance to the imperial crown, and perhaps
not to the perfon of the King ; as the title to the crown is
derived from an act of parliament, made fince the fettlement of this province, which act refpects the imperial
crown only.   Let us wave this difficulty, and fuppofe allegiance due from the colonies to the perfon of the king of
Great Britain ; he then appears in a new capacity, as king
of America, or rather, in feveral new capacities, as king of
Maffachufetts, king of Rhode-Ifland, king of Connecticut,
&c. &c. For, if our connection with Great Britain, by the
parliament, be diffolved, we fhall have none among ourfelves ;
but each colony will become as diftinct from the others,
as England was from Scotland before the union.   Some
have fuppofed, that each ftate having one and the fame
perfon for its king, it is a fufficient connection: Were he an
abfolute monarch, it might be ; but, in a mixed government, it is no union at all.   For, as the king muft govern
each ftate by its parliament, thofe feveral parliaments would
purfue the particular intereft of its own ftate ; and however
well difpofed the king might be to purfue a line of intereft
that was common to all, the checks and controul, that he
would meet with, would render it impoffible. If the king

G   of

of Great-Britain has really thefe new capacities, they ought
to be added to his titles ; and then another difficulty will
arife, the prerogatives of thefe new crowns have never been
defined or limited. Is the monarchical part of the feveral
provincial conftitutions to be nearer, or more remote from
abfolute monarchy, in an inverted ratio to each one's approaching to, or receding from a republic ? But let us
fuppofe the fame prerogatives inherent in the feveral American crowns, as are in the imperial crown of Great-Britain; where fhall we find the Britifh conftitution, that we all
agree we are entitled to ? We fhall feek for it in vain in
our provincial affemblies. They are but faint fketches of
the eftates of parliament. The houfes of reprefentatives or
burgeffes have not all the powers of the houfe of commons:
in the charter governments they have no more than what
is exprefsly granted by their feveral charters. The firft
charters, granted to this province, did not impower the affembly to tax the people at all. Our council-boards are as
deftitute of the conftitutional authority of the houfe of
lords, as their feveral members are of the noble independence and fplendid appendages of peerage. The houfe of
peers is the bulwark of the Britifh conftitution, and, thro'
fucceffive ages, has withftood the fhocks of monarchy, and
the fappings of democracy, whilft the conftitution gained
ftrength by the conflict. Thus, the fuppofition of our being independent ftates, or exempt from the authority of
parliament, deftroys the very idea of our having a Britifh
conftitution. The provincial conftitutions, confidered as
fubordinate, are generally well adapted to thofe purpofes
of government, for which they were intended, that is, to
regulate the internal police of the feveral colonies ; but,
having no principle of ftability within themfelves, tho' they
may fupport themfelves in moderate times, they would be
merged by the violence of turbulent ones. The feveral colonies would become wholly monarchical or wholly republican,
were it not for the checks, controuls, regulations and fup-
ports, of the fupreme authority of the empire. Thus, the
argument that is drawn from their firft principle of our
being entitled to Englifh liberties, deftroys the principle itfelf; it deprives us of the bill of rights, and all the benefits

re-

refulting from the revolution, of Englifh laws, and of the Britifh conftitution.

Our patriots have been fo intent upon building up A-merican rights, that they have overlooked the rights of Great Britain, and our own intereft. Inftead of proving, that we were entitled to privileges which our fathers knew our fituation would not admit us to enjoy, they have been arguing away our moft effential rights. If there be any grievance, it does not confift in our being fubject to the authority of parliament, but in our not having an actual reprefentation in it. Were it poffible for the colonies to have an equal reprefentation in parliament, and were re-fufed it upon proper application, I confefs, I fhould think it a grievance : But, at prefent it feems to be allowed, by all parties, to be impracticable, confidering that the colonies are diftant from Great-Britain a thoufand tranfmarine leagues. If that be the cafe, the right or privilege that we complain of being deprived of, is not withheld by Britain ; but the firft principles of government, and the immutable laws of nature, render it impoffible for us to enjoy it. This is ap-parently the meaning of that celebrated paffage in Gover-nor Hutchinfon's letter, that rang through the continent, viz. There muft be an abridgement of what is called Eng-lifh liberties. He fubjoins, that he had never yet feen the projection, whereby a colony, three thoufand miles from the parent-ftate, might enjoy all the privileges of *that* pa-rent-ftate and be fubject to it, or in words to that effect. The obnoxious fentence, taken detached from the letter, appears very unfriendly to the colonies ; but, confidered in connection with the other parts of the letter, is but a neceffary refult from our fituation. Allegiance and pro-tection are reciprocal. It is our higheft intereft to conti-nue a part of the Britifh empire, and equally our duty to remain fubject to the authority of parliament. Our own internal police may generally be regulated by our provin-cial legiflatures ; but, in national concerns, or where our own affemblies do not anfwer the ends of government, with refpect to ourfelves, the ordinances or interpofition of the great council of the nation is neceffary. In this cafe,

the

the major mu{t} rule the minor. After many more centuries {$\int$}hall have rolled away, long after we, who are now bu{$\int$}tling upon the {$\int$}tage of life, {$\int$}hall have been received to the bo{$\int$}om of mother earth, and our names are forgotten ; the colonies may be {$\int$}o far encrea{$\int$}ed as to have the balance of wealth, numbers, and power in their favour. The good of the empire may then make it nece{$\int$}{$\int$}ary to fix the {$\int$}eat of government here ; and {$\int$}ome future GEORGE, equally the friend of mankind with him who now {$\int$}ways the Briti{$\int$}h {$\int$}ceptre, may cro{$\int$}s the Atlantic, and rule Great Britain by an American parliament.

MASSACHUSETTENSIS.

January 9, 1775.

LETTER VI.

To the Inhabitants of the Province of Ma{$\int$}{$\int$}achu{$\int$}etts-Bay.

HAD a per{$\int$}on, {$\int$}ome fifteen years ago, undertaken to prove that the colonies were a part of the Briti{$\int$}h empire or dominion, and, as {$\int$}uch, {$\int$}ubje{$\hat c$}t to the authority of the Briti{$\int$}h parliament; he would have a{$\hat c$}ted as ridiculous a part, as to have undertaken to prove a {$\int$}elf-evident propo{$\int$}ition : Had any per{$\int$}on denied it, he would have been called a fool or madman. At this wi{$\int$}e period, individuals and bodies of men deny it, notwith{$\int$}tanding in doing it they {$\int$}ubvert the fundamentals of government, deprive us of Briti{$\int$}h liberties, and build up ab{$\int$}olute monarchy in the colonies; for our charters {$\int$}uppo{$\int$}e regal authority in the grantor. If that authority be derived from the Briti{$\int$}h crown, it præ-{$\int$}uppo{$\int$}es this territory to have been a part of the Briti{$\int$}h dominion, and as {$\int$}uch {$\int$}ubje{$\hat c$}t to the imperial {$\int$}overeign. If that authority was ve{$\int$}ted in the per{$\int$}on of the King, in a different capacity; the Briti{$\int$}h con{$\int$}titution and laws are out of the que{$\int$}tion, and the King mu{$\int$}t be as ab{$\int$}olute to us, as tho' his prerogatives had never been circum{$\int$}cribed. Such mu{$\int$}t have been the {$\int$}overeign authority of the {$\int$}everal Kings, who have granted American charters, previous to the {$\int$}everal grants: there is nothing to detra{$\hat c$}t from it, at this time in tho{$\int$}e colonies that are de{$\int$}titute of charters; and

the

the charter governments muſt then ſeverally revert to abſolute monarchy as their charters may happen to be forfeited by the grantees not fulfilling the conditions of them, for
every charter contains an expreſs or implied condition.

It is curious indeed to trace the denial and oppugnation
to the ſupreme authority of the ſtate. When the ſtamp-
act was made, the authority of parliament to impoſe internal taxes was denied, but their right to impoſe external
ones, or, in other words, to lay duties upon goods and
merchandiſe, was admitted. When the act was made, im-
poſing duties upon tea, &c. a new diſtinction was ſet up ;
that the parliament had a right to lay duties upon merchandiſe for the purpoſe of regulating trade, but not for
the purpoſe of raiſing a revenue. That is, the parliament
had good right and lawful authority to lay the former
duty of a ſhilling on the pound, but had none to lay the
preſent duty of three pence. Having got thus far ſafe, it
was only taking one ſtep more to extricate ourſelves en-
tirely from their fangs, and become independent ſtates :
That our patriots moſt heroically reſolved upon, and flatly
denied that parliament had a right to make any laws whatever, that ſhould be binding upon the colonies. There
is no poſſible medium between abſolute independence and
ſubjection to the authority of parliament. He muſt be
blind indeed that cannot ſee our deareſt intereſt in the
latter, notwithſtanding many pant after the former : miſ-
guided men! could they once overtake their wiſh, they
would be convinced of the madneſs of the purſuit.

My dear countrymen, it is of the laſt importance that
we ſettle this point clearly in our minds ; it will ſerve as a
ſure teſt, certain criterion, and invariable ſtandard, to diſtin-
guiſh the friends from the enemies of our country, patriot-
iſm from ſedition, loyalty from rebellion. To deny the
ſupreme authority of the ſtate is a high miſdemeanor, to
ſay no worſe of it ; to oppoſe it by force is an overt act
of treaſon, puniſhable by confiſcation of eſtate and a moſt
ignominious death. The realm of England is an appro-
priate term for the ancient realm of England, in contra-
diſtinction to Wales and other territories that have been
an-

annexed to it. Thefe, as they have been feverally annexed to the crown, whether by conqueft or otherwile, became a part of the empire, and fubject to the authority of parliament, whether they fend members to parliament or not, and whether they have legiflative powers of their own or not.

Thus Ireland, which has perhaps the greateft poffible fubordinate legiflature, and fends no members to the Britifh parliament, is bound by its acts, when exprefsly named. Guernfey and Jerfey are no part of the realm of England, nor are they reprefented in parliament, but are fubject to its authority: And, in the fame predicament are the American colonies, and all the other difperfions of the empire. Permit me to requeft your attention to this fubject a little longer: I affure you it is as interefting and important, as it is dry and unentertaining.

Let us now recur to the firft charter of this province, and we fhall find irrefiftable evidence, that our being part of the empire, fubject to the fupreme authority of the ftate, bound by its laws and entitled to its protection, were the terms and conditions by which our anceftors held their lands and fettled the province. Our charter, like all other American charters, is under the great feal of England; the grants are made by the King, for his heirs and *fuccefors*, the feveral tenures to be of the King, his heirs and *fucceffors:* in like manner are the refervations. It is apparent, the King acted in his royal capacity, as King of England, which neceffarily fuppofes the territory granted, to be a part of the Englifh dominions, holden of the crown of England.

The charter, after reciting feveral grants of the territory to Sir Henry Rofwell and others, proceeds to incorporation in thefe words : ' And for as much as the good and prof-' perous fuccefs of the plantations of the faid parts of New-' England aforefaid intended by the faid Sir Henry Rofwell ' and others, to be fpeedily fet upon, cannot but chiefly ' depend, next under the bleffing of almighty God and the ' fupport of our royal authority, upon the good govern-' ment of the fame, to the end that the *affairs of bufinefs,* ' which

' which from time to time fhall happen and arife concern-
' ing the faid lands and the plantations of the fame may be
' the better managed and ordered, we have further hereby,
' of our fpecial grace, certain knowledge and meer motion,
' given, granted and confirmed, and for us, our heirs and
' fucceffors, do give, grant and confirm unto our faid trufty
' and well beloved fubjects, Sir Henry Rofwell, &c. and
' all fuch others as fhall hereafter be admitted and made
' free of *the company and fociety hereafter mentioned,* fhall
' from time to time and at all times, forever hereafter, be,
' by virtue of thefe prefents, *one body corporate, politic in*
' *fact and name, by the name of the Governor and company*
' *of the Maffachufetts-Bay, in New-England*; and them
' by the name of the Governor and company of the Maf-
' fachufetts-Bay, in New-England, one body politic and
' corporate in deed, fact and name. We do for us, our
' heirs and fucceffors make, ordain, conftitute and confirm
' by thefe prefents, and that by that name they fhall have
' perpetual fucceffion, and that by that name they and their
' fucceffors fhall be capable and enabled as well *to implead*
' *and to be impleaded, and to profecute, demand and anfwer and*
' *be anfwered unto all and fingular fuits, caufes, quarrels and*
' *actions of what kind or nature foever; and alfo to have, take,*
' *poffefs, acquire and purchafe, any lands, tenements and he-*
' *reditaments, or any goods or chattles, the fame to leafe, grant,*
' *demife, aliene, bargain, fell and difpofe of, as our liege people*
' *of this our realm of England, or any other corporation or body*
' *politic of the fame, may do.*' I would beg leave to afk one
fimple queftion, whether this looks like a diftinct ftate or
independent empire. Provifion is then made for electing a
governor, deputy governor and eighteen affiftants. After
which is this claufe: ' We do for us, our heirs and fuccef-
' fors, give and grant to the faid governor and company
' and their fucceffors, that the governor, or in his abfence
' the deputy-governor, of the faid company for the time
' being, and fuch of the affiftants or freemen of the faid
' company as fhall be prefent, or the greater number of
' them fo affembled, whereof the governor or deputy-
' governor and fix of the affiftants, at the leaft to be feven,
                                                              fhall

' fhall have full power and authority to choofe, nominate
' and appoint fuch and fo many others, as they fhall think
' fit, and fhall be willing to accept the fame to be free of
' the faid company and body, and them into the fame to
' admit and to elect and conftitute fuch officers as they
' fhall think fit and requifite for the ordering, managing
' and difpatching of the affairs of the faid governor and
' company and their fucceffors, and to make *laws and or-*
' *dinances for the good and welfare of the faid company,* and
' for the government and ordering of the faid lands and
' plantations and the people inhabiting and to inhabit the
' fame, as to them from time to time fhall be thought
' meet : *So as fuch laws and ordinances be not contrary or re-*
' *pugnant to the laws and ftatutes of this our realm of England.*'
  Another claufe is this ; ' And for their further encou-
' ragement, of our efpecial grace and favour, we do by
' thefe prefents, for us, our heirs, and fucceffors, yield
' and grant to the faid governor and company and their
' fucceffors, and every one of them, their factors and af-
' figns, that they and every of them fhall be free and quit
' from all taxes, fubfidies and cuftoms in New-England
' for the fpace of feven years, and from all taxes and im-
' pofitions for the fpace of twenty-one years, upon all goods
' and merchandize, at any time or times hereafter, either
' upon importation thither, or exportation from thence into
' our realm of England, or into other of our dominions,
' by the faid governor and company and their fucceffors,
' their deputies, factors and affigns, &c.'
  The exemption from taxes for feven years in one cafe,
and twenty one years in the other, plainly indicates that,
after their expiration, this province would be liable to taxation. Now I would afk, by what authority thofe taxes
were to be impofed ? It could not be by the governor and
company, for no fuch power was delegated or granted to
them ; and befides it would have been abfurd and nugatory
to exempt them from their own taxation, fuppofing them
to have had the power, for they might have exempted
themfelves.—It muft therefore be by the King or parliament : it could not be by the *King alone,* for as King of
Eng-

England, the political capacity in which he granted the
charter, he had no such power, exclusive of the lords and
commons, consequently it must have been by the parliament. This clause in the charter is as evident a recogni-
tion of the authority of the parliament over this province,
as if the words, " acts of parliament, " had been inserted,
as they were in the Pennsylvania charter. There was no
session of parliament after the grant of our charter until the
year 1640.—In 1642 the house of commons passed a resolve, ' that, for the better advancement of the plantations
' in New-England, and the encouragement of the planters
' to proceed in their undertaking, their exports and im-
' ports should be freed and discharged from all customs,
' subsidies, taxations and duties, until the further order of
' the house. ' Which was gratefully received and recorded
in the archives of our predecessors.—This transaction shews
very clearly in what sense our connection with England
was then understood. It is true that, in some arbitrary
reigns, attempts were made by the servants of the crown
to exclude the two houses of parliament, from any share
of the authority over the colonies; they also attempted to
render the King absolute in England: but the parliament
always rescued the colonies, as well as England, from such
attempts.

I shall recite but one more clause of this charter, which
is this, ' And further our will and pleasure is, and we do
' hereby for us, our heirs and successors, ordain, declare
' and grant to the said govenor and company, and their
' successors, that all and every of the subjects of us, our
' heirs and successors, which shall go to and inhabit within
' the said land and premises hereby mentioned to be grant-
' ed, and every of their children, which shall happen to be
' born there, or on the seas in going thither, or returning
' from thence, shall have and enjoy *all liberties and immuni-*
' *ties of free and natural subjects, within any of the dominions*
' of us, our heirs or successors, to all intents, constructions
' and purposes whatsoever, as if they and every of them
' were born within the realm of England. ' It is upon
this or a similar clause in the charter of William and

H   Mary

Mary, that our patriots have built up the ſtupendous fabric of American independence. They argue from it a total exemption from parliamentary authority, becauſe we are not repreſented in parliament.

I have already ſhewn, that the ſuppoſition of our being exempt from the authority of parliament, is pregnant with the groſſeſt abſurdities. Let us now conſider this clauſe in connection with the other parts of the charter. It is a rule of law, founded in reaſon and common ſenſe, to conſtrue each part of an inſtrument, ſo as the whole may hang together, and be conſiſtent with itſelf. If we ſuppoſe this clauſe to exempt us from the authority of parliament, we muſt throw away all the reſt of the charter; for every other part indicates the contrary, as plainly as words can do it, and, what is ſtill worſe, this clauſe becomes *felo de ſe*, and deſtroys itſelf; for if we are not annexed to the crown, we are aliens, and no charter, grant or other act of the crown, can naturalize us or entitle us to the liberties and immunities of Engliſhmen. It can be done only by act of parliament. An alien is one born in a ſtrange country, out of the allegiance of the King, and is under many diſabilities though reſiding in the realm. As Wales, Jerſey, Guernſey, Ireland, the foreign plantations, &c. were ſeverally annexed to the crown, they became parts of one and the ſame empire, the natives of which are equally free as though they had been born in that territory, which was the antient realm. As our patriots depend upon this clauſe, detached from the charter, let us view it in that light. If a perſon, born in England, remove to Ireland, and ſettle there, he is then no longer repreſented in the Britiſh parliament; but he and his poſterity are and will ever be ſubject to the authority of the Britiſh parliament: If he remove to Jerſey, Guernſey, or any other parts of the Britiſh dominions that ſend no members to parliament, he will ſtill be in the ſame predicament. So that the inhabitants of the American colonies do in fact enjoy all the liberties and immunities of natural-born ſubjects. We are entitled to no greater privileges than thoſe, that are born within the realm; and they can enjoy no other than

we

we do, when they reside out of it. Thus, it is evident, that this clause amounts to no more than the royal assurance, that we are a part of the British empire, are not aliens, but natural-born subjects, and, as such, bound to obey the supreme power of the state, and entitled to protection from it. To avoid prolixity, I shall not remark particularly upon other parts of this charter, but observe in general, that whoever reads it with attention will meet with irresistable evidence in every part of it, that our being a part of the English dominions, subject to the English crown, and within the jurisdiction of parliament, were the terms upon which our ancestors settled this colony, and the very tenures by which they held their estates.

No lands within the British dominions are perfectly allodial; they are held mediately or immediately of the King, and, upon forfeiture, revert to the crown. My dear countrymen, you have many of you been most falsly and wickedly told, by our patriots, that Great-Britain was meditating a land tax, and seeking to deprive us of our inheritance; but had all the malice and subtilty of men and devils been united, a readier method to effect it could not have been devised, than the late denials of the authority of parliament, and forcible oppositions to its acts : Yet, this has been planned and executed chiefly by persons of *desperate* fortunes.

MASSACHUSETTENSIS.

January 16, 1775.

LETTER VII.

To the Inhabitants of the Province of Massachusetts Bay.

IF we carry our researches further back than the emigration of our ancestors, we shall find many things that reflect light upon the object we are in quest of. It is immaterial when America was first discovered or taken possession of by the English. In 1602 one *Gosnold* landed upon one of the islands, called Elizabeth-islands, which were so named in honor of Queen Elizabeth, built a fort and projected a settlement; but his men were discouraged,

and

and the project failed. In 1606 King James granted all
the continent from 34 to 45 degrees, which he divided
into two colonies, viz. the southern or Virginia, to certain merchants at London; the northern or New-England,
to certain merchants at Plymouth in England. In 1607
some of the patentees of the northern colony began a settlement at Sagadahoc, but the emigrants were disheart-
ened after the trial of one winter, and that attempt failed
of success. Thus this territory had not only been granted
by the crown for purposes of colonization, which are to
enlarge the empire or dominion of the parent state, and
to open new sources of national wealth; but actual possession had been taken by the grantees, previous to the emigration of our ancestors, or any grant to them. In 1620
a patent was granted to the adventurers for the northern
colony, incorporating them by the name of *the council for
the affairs of New-Plymouth.* From this company of merchants in England, our ancestors derived their title to this
territory. The tract of land called Massachusetts was purchased of this company by Sir Henry Roswell and asso-
ciates: their deed bears date, March 19th, 1627. In 1628
they obtained a charter of incorporation, which I have
already remarked upon. The liberties, privileges and
franchises, granted by this charter, do not, perhaps, exceed those granted to the city of London and other corporations within the realm. The legislative power was
very confined; it did not even extend to levying taxes of
any kind: that power was, however, assumed under this
charter, which by law worked a forfeiture, and for this
among other things, in the reign of Charles the Second,
the charter was adjudged forfeited, and the franchises seiz-
ed into the King's hands. This judgment did not affect
our ancestors' title to their lands, which were not derived
originally from the charter, though confirmed by it, but
by purchase from the council at Plymouth, who held
immediately under the crown. Besides, our ancestors had
now reduced what before was a naked right to possession,
and by persevering through unequalled toils, hardships
and dangers, at the approach of which other emigrants
had

had fainted, rendered New-England a very valuable acquifition both to the crown and nation. This was highly meritorious, and ought not to be overlooked in ad-
jufting the prefent unhappy difpute; but our patriots
would deprive us of all the merit, both to the crown
and nation, by *fevering us from* BOTH. After the revolution, our anceftors petitioned the parliament to reftore the charter. A bill for that purpofe paffed the
houfe of commons, but went no further. In confequence of another petition, King William and Queen
Mary granted our prefent charter for uniting and incorporating the Maffachufetts, New-Plymouth, and feveral other territories into one province. More extenfive powers of legiflation, than thofe contained in the
firft charter, were become neceffary, and were granted.
And the form of the legiflature was made to approach
nearer to the form of the fupreme legiflature. The
powers of legiflation are confined to local or provincial
purpofes, and further reftricted by thefe words, viz. *So
as the fame be not repugnant or contrary to the laws of
this our realm of England.* Our patriots have made
many nice diftinctions and curious refinements to evade
the force of thefe words; but, after all, it is impoffible
to reconcile them to the idea of an independent ftate,
as it is to reconcile difability to omnipotence. The
provincial power of taxation is alfo reftricted to provincial purpofes, and allowed to be exercifed over fuch
only, as are inhabitants or proprietors within the province. I would obferve here, that the granting *fubordinate* powers of legiflation, does not abridge or dimi-
nifh the powers of the *higher* legiflatures: thus we
fee corporations in England and the feveral towns in
this province vefted with greater or leffer powers of legiflation, without the parliament, in one cafe, or the general court in the other; being reftrained from enacting
thofe very laws, that fall within the jurifdiction of the feveral corporations. Had our prefent charter been conceived in fuch equivocal terms, as that it might be conftrued
as reftraining the authority of parliament; the uniform
usage

usage, ever since it passed the seal, would satisfy us that its intent was different. The parliament in the reign when it was granted, long before and in every reign since, has been making statutes to extend to the colonies; and those statutes have been as uniformly submitted to, as authoritative, by the colonies, till within ten or a dozen years. Sometimes acts of parliament have been made, and sometimes have been repealed, in consequence of petitions from the colonies. The provincial assemblies often refer to acts of parliament in their own, and have sometimes made acts to aid their execution. It is evident that it was the intention of their Majesties to grant subordinate powers of legislation, without impairing or diminishing the authority of the supreme legislature. Had there been any words in the charter, which precluded that construction, or did the whole taken together contradict it; lawyers would tell us, that the King was deceived in his grant, and the patentees took no estate by it, because the crown can neither alienate a part of the British dominions, nor impair the supreme power of the empire. I have dwelt longer on this subject than I at first intended, and not by any means done it justice; as, to avoid prolix narratives and tedious deduction, I have omitted perhaps more than I have adduced, in order to evince the truth of the position, that we are a part of the British dominions, and subject to the authority of parliament. The novelty of the contrary tenets will appear, by extracting a part of a pamphlet, published in 1764, by a Boston gentleman, who was then the oracle of the whigs, and whose profound knowledge in the law and constitution is equalled but by few.

‘ I also lay it down (says he) as one of the first principles
‘ from whence I intend to deduce the civil rights of the British
‘ colonies, that all of them are subject to, and dependent on
‘ Great-Britain; and that therefore, as over subordinate
‘ governments, the parliament has an undoubted power and
‘ lawful authority to make acts for the general good, that, by
‘ naming them, shall and ought to be equally binding, as
‘ upon the subjects of Great-Britain within the realm. Is
‘ there the least difference, as to the consent of the colonists,
‘whether

' whether taxes and impofitions are laid on their trade, and
' other property by the crown alone, or by the parliament ?
' As it is agreed on all hands, the crown alone cannot im-
' pofe them, we fhould be juftifiable in refufing to pay
' them ; *but we muſt and ought to yield obedience to an act of*
' *parliament, though erroneous, till repealed.*

' It is a maxim, that the King can do no wrong; and
' every good fubject is bound to believe his King is not
' inclined to do any. We are bleſſed with a prince who
' has given abundant demonſtrations, that, in all his actions,
' he ſtudies the good of his people, and the true glory of
' his crown, which are infeparable. It would therefore be
' the higheft degree of impudence and difloyalty, to imagine
' that the King, at the head of his parliament, could have
' any but the moſt pure and perfect intentions of juſtice,
' goodneſs and truth, that human nature is capable of.
' All this I fay and believe of the King and parliament, in
' all their acts ; even in that which fo nearly affects the
' interefts of the coloniſts ; and that a moſt perfect and
' ready obedience is to be yielded to it while it remains in
' force. The power of parliament is uncontrolable but
' by themfelves, and we muſt obey. They only can re-
' peal their own acts. There would be an end of all go-
' vernment, if one or a number of fubjects, or fubordinate
' provinces, fhould take upon them fo far to judge of the
' juſtice of an act of parliament, as to refufe obedience to
' it. If there was nothing elfe to reſtrain fuch a ſtep, pru-
' dence ought to do it ; for forcibly refiſting the parliament
' and the King's laws is high-treafon. Therefore let the
' parliament lay what burdens they pleafe on us, we muſt,
' it is our duty to fubmit and patiently bear them, till they
' will be pleafed to relieve us.'

The Pennfylvania Farmer, who took the lead in ex-
plaining away the right of parliament to raife a revenue in
America, fpeaking of regulating trade, tells us, that ' He
' who confiders thefe provinces as *ſtates diſtinct from the*
' *Britiſh empire* has very flender notions of *juſtice* or of *their*
' *intereſt* ; we are but *parts of a whole*, and therefore there
' muſt exiſt a power fomewhere to *prefide and preferve the*

' *connection in due order.* This power is lodged in parlia-
' ment ; and we are as much *dependent on Great-Britain* as
' a *perfectly free people could be on another.*' He supposes that
we are dependent in some considerable degree upon Great-
Britain ; and that such dependance is nevertheless consistent with perfect freedom.

Having settled this point, let us reflect upon the resolves
and proceedings of our patriots. We often read resolves
denying the authority of parliament; which is the imperial
authority, gilded over with professions of loyalty to the
King, but the golden leaf is too thin to conceal the treason.: It either argues profound ignorance or hypocritical
cunning.

We find many unsuspecting persons prevailed on openly
to oppose the execution of acts of parliament with force
and arms. My friends ! some of the persons, that beguiled
you, could have turned to the chapter, page and section,
where such insurrections are pronounced rebellions, by the
law of the land ; and had not their hearts been dead to a
sense of justice, and steeled against every feeling of humanity, they would have timely warned you of your danger.
Our patriots have sent us in pursuit of a mere *ignis fatuus,*
a fascinating glare devoid of substance; and now, when we
find ourselves bewildered, with scarce one ray of hope to
raise our sinking spirits, or stay our fainting souls, they
conjure up phantoms more delusive and fleeting, if possible, than that which first led us astray. They tell us, we
are a *match* for Great-Britain.—The twentieth part of the
strength that Great-Britain could exert, were it necessary,
is more than sufficient to crush this defenceless province to
atoms, notwithstanding all the vapouring of the disaffected
here and elsewhere. They tell us the army is disaffected to
the service : What pains have our politicians not taken to
attach them to the service ? The officers conceive no very
favourable opinion of the cause of the whigs, from the oblo-
quy with which their General hath been treated, in return
for his humanity ; nor from the infamous attempts to seduce
the soldiers from his Majesty's service. The policy of some
of our patriots has been as weak and contemptible, as their
motives

motives are fordid and malevolent; for when they found
their fuccefs in corrupting the foldiery did not anfwer
their expectations, they took pains to attach them the
firmer to the caufe they adhered to, by preventing the
erecting of barracks for their winter quarters; by which
means many contracted difeafes, and fome lives were loft,
from the unwholefome buildings they were obliged to occupy. And, as though fome ftimulus was ftill wanting,
fome provocation to prevent human nature revolting in the
hour of battle, they deprived the foldiers of a gratification
never denied to the brute creation,—ftraw to lay on. I do
not mention this conduct to raife the refentment of the
troops; it has had its effect already, and it is proper you
fhould know it; nor fhould I have blotted paper in re-
lating facts fo mortifying to the pride of man, had it not
been bafely fuggefted, that there would be a defection fhould
the army take the field. Thofe are matters of fmall moment compared to another, which is *the caufe* they are engaged in. It is no longer a ftruggle between whigs and
tories, whether thefe or thofe fhall occupy pofts of honor,
or enjoy the emoluments of office; nor is it now whether
this or the other act of parliament fhall be repealed. The
army is fent here to decide a queftion, intimately connected with the honor and intereft of the nation; no lefs than
whether the colonies fhall continue a part of, or be for ever
difmembered from, the Britifh empire. It is a caufe in which
no honeft American can wifh our politicians fuccefs,
though it is devoutly to be wifhed, that their difcomfiture
may be effected without recourfe being had to the *ultima
ratio*,—the fword. This our wretched fituation is but the
natural confequence of denying the authority of parliament
and forcibly oppofing its acts.

Sometimes we are amufed with intimations, that Holland,
France, or Spain, will make a diverfion in our favour.—
Thefe, equally with the others, are fuggeftions of defpair.
Thefe powers have colonies of their own, and might not
choofe to fet a bad example, by encouraging the colonies
of any other ftate to revolt. The Dutch have too much
money in the Englifh funds, and are too much attached to

I   their

their money, to efpoufe our quarrel. The French and Spaniards have not yet forgot the drubbing they received from Great-Britain laft war ; and all three fear to offend that power, which our politicians would perfuade us to defpife.

Laftly, they tell us, that he people in England will take our part, and prevent matters from coming to extremity. This *is* their fort, where, when driven from every other poft, they fly for refuge.

Alas ! my friends, our congreffes have ftopped up every avenue that leads to that fanctuary. We hear, by every arrival from England, that it is no longer a minifterial (if it ever was) but a national caufe. My dear countrymen, I deal plainly with you ; I never fhould forgive myfelf if I did not. Are there not eleven regiments in Bofton ? A refpectable fleet in the harbour ? Men of war ftationed at every confiderable port along the continent ? Are there not three fhips of the line fent here, notwithftanding the danger of the winter coaft, with more than the ufual compliment of marines ? Have not our congreffes, county, provincial and continental, inftead of making advances for an accommodation, bid defiance to Great-Britain ?—*He that runs may read.*

If our politicians will not be perfuaded from running againft the thick boffes of the buckler, it is time for us to leave them to their fate, and provide for the fafety of ourfelves, our wives, our children, our friends, and our country.

I have many things to add, but muft now take my leave, for this week, by fubmitting to your judgment, whether there be not an abfolute neceffity of immediately protefting againft all traiterous refolves, leagues and affociations, of bodies of men, that appear to have acted in a reprefentative capacity. Had our congreffes been accidental or fpontaneous meetings, the whole might have refted upon the individuals that compofed them ; but as they appear in the character of the peoples delegates, is there not the utmoft danger of the innocent being confounded with the guilty, unlefs they take timely care to diftinguifh themfelves ?

MASSACHUSETTENSIS.

January 23, 1775.   LET-

L E T T E R VIII.

To the Inhabitants of the Province of Maſſachuſetts-Bay.

AS the oppugnation to the King in parliament tends manifeſtly to independence, and the colonies would ſoon arrive at that point, did not Great-Britain check them in their career ; let us indulge the idea, however extravagant and romantic, and ſuppoſe ourſelves for ever ſeparated from the parent-ſtate. Let us ſuppoſe Great-Britain ſinking under the violence of the ſhock, and overwhelmed by her antient hereditary enemies ; or, what is more probable, opening new ſources of national wealth, to ſupply the deficiency of that which uſed to flow to her through American channels, and perhaps planting more loyal colonies in the new diſcovered regions of the ſouth, ſtill retaining her præ-eminence among the nations, though regardleſs of America.

Let us new advert to our own ſituation. Deſtitute of Britiſh protection, that impervious barrier, behind which, in perfect ſecurity, we have increaſed to a degree almoſt exceeding the bounds of probability ; what other Britain could we look to, when in diſtreſs ?—What ſuccedaneum does the world afford, to make good the loſs ? Would not our trade, navigation and fiſhery, which no nation dares violate or invade, while diſtinguiſhed by Britiſh colours, become the ſport and prey of the maritime powers of Europe ? Would not our maritime towns be expoſed to the pillaging of every piratical enterprize ? Are the colonies able to maintain a fleet, ſufficient to afford one idea of ſecurity to ſuch an extenſive ſea-coaſt ? Before they can defend themſelves againſt foreign invaſions, they muſt unite into one empire ; otherwiſe the jarring intereſts, and oppoſite propenſities, would render the many headed monſter in politics unweildy and inactive. Neither the *form* or *ſeat* of government would be readily agreed upon ; more difficult ſtill would it be to fix upon the *perſon* or *perſons,* to be inveſted with the imperial authority. There is perhaps as great a diverſity between the tempers and habits of the inhabitants of this province, and the tempers and habits

bits

bits of the Carolinians, as there fubfift between fome different nations: nor need we travel fo far; the Rhode-Ifland-
ers are as unlike the people of Connecticut, as thofe
mentioned before. Moft of the colonies are rivals to each
other in trade. Between others there fubfift deep animofities, refpecting their boundaries, which have heretofore
produced violent altercations; and the fword of civil war
has been more than once unfheathed, without bringing
thefe difputes to a decifion. It is apparent, that fo many
difcordant heterogeneous particles could not fuddenly unite
and confolidate into one body: It is moft probable, that, if
they were ever united, the union would be effected by fome
afpiring genius, putting himfelf at the head of the colonifts
army (for we muft fuppofe a very refpectable one indeed before we are fevered from Britain), who, taking advantage of
the enfeebled, bleeding and diftracted ftate of the colonies,
would fubjugate the whole to the yoke of defpotifm. Human nature is every where the fame; and this has often been
the iffue of thofe rebellions that the rightful prince was unable to fubdue. We need not travel through the ftates of
antient Greece and Rome, or the more modern ones in Europe, to pick up the inftances, with which the way is
ftrewed; we have a notable one in our own. So odious
and arbitrary was the protectorate of *Cromwell*, that when
death had delivered them from the dread of the tyrant,
all parties confpired to reftore monarchy, and each one
ftrove to be the foremoft in inviting home and placing upon
the imperial throne, their exiled prince, the fon of the
fame Charles, who, not many years before, had been
murdered on a fcaffold. The republicans themfelves now
rufhed to the oppofite extreme; and had Charles the fecond
been as induftrious, as fome of his predeceffors were, he
might have eftablifhed in England a power more arbitrary
than the firft Charles ever had in contemplation.

Let us now fuppofe the colonies united and moulded
into fome form of government. Think one moment of the
revenue neceffary both to fupport this government and to
provide for even the appearance of defence. Conceive
yourfelves in a manner exhaufted by the conflict with
Great-

Great-Britain, now ſtaggering and ſinking under the load
of your own taxes, and the weight of your own government. Conſider further, that to render government ope-
rative and ſalutary, *ſubordination* is neceſſary. This our
patriots need not be told of; and when once they had
mounted the ſteed, and found themſelves ſo well ſeated as
to run no riſk of being thrown from the ſaddle, the ſeverity
of their diſcipline to reſtore ſubordination, would be in
proportion to their former treachery in deſtroying it. We
have already ſeen ſpecimens of their tyranny, in their in-
human treatment of perſons guilty of no crime, except
that of differing in ſentiment from themſelves. What then
muſt we expect from ſuch ſcourges of mankind, when ſupported by imperial power?

To elude the difficulty, reſulting from our defenceleſs
ſituation, we are told, that the colonies would open a free
trade with all the world, and all nations would join in protecting their common mart. A very little reflection will
convince us that this is chimerical. American trade, however beneficial to Great-Britain, while ſhe can command
it, would be but as a drop of the bucket, or the light duſt
of the balance, to all the commercial ſtates of Europe.
Beſides, were Britiſh fleets and armies no longer deſtined
to our protection, in a very ſhort time France and Spain
would recover poſſeſſion of thoſe territories, that were
torn, reluctant and bleeding from them, in the laſt war, by
the ſuperior ſtrength of Britain. Our enemies would again
extend their line of fortification, from the northern to the
ſouthern ſhore, and by means of our late ſettlements ſtretch-
ing themſelves to the confines of Canada, and the communication opened from one country to the other, we
ſhould be expoſed to perpetual incurſions from Canadians
and ſavages; but our diſtreſs would not end here, for
when once theſe incurſions ſhould be ſupported by the
formidable armaments of France and Spain, the whole
continent would become their eaſy prey, and would be
parcelled out, Poland like. Recollect the conſternation
we were thrown into laſt war, when Fort-William Henry
was taken by the French: It was apprehended that all
New-

New-England would be over-run by their conquering arms. It was even propofed, for our own people to burn and lay wafte all the country weft of Connecticut river, to impede the enemies march, and prevent their ravaging the country eaft of it. This propofal came from no inconfiderable man. Confider what muft *really* have been our fate, unaided by Britain laft war.

Great-Britain afide, what earthly power ccould ftretch out the compaffionate arm to fhield us from thofe powers, that have long beheld us with the fharp, piercing eyes of avidity, and have heretofore bled freely and expended their millions to obtain us ? Do you fuppofe their luft of empire is fatiated ? Or do you fuppofe they would fcorn to obtain fo glorious a prize by an eafy conqueft ? Or can any be fo vifionary or impious as to believe that the Father of the univerfe will work miracles in favour of rebellion, and, after having by fome unfeen arm and mighty power deftroyed Great-Britain for us, will in the fame myfterious way defend us againft other European powers ? Sometimes we are told, that the colonies may put themfelves under the protection of fome one foreign ftate ; but it ought to be confidered that, to do that, we muft throw ourfelves into their power. We can make them no return for protection but by trade, and of that they can have no affurance, *unlefs we become fubject to their laws* ; this is evident by our contention with Britain.

Which ftate would you prefer being annexed to, France, Spain, or Holland ? I fuppofe the latter, as it is a republic : but are you fure, that the other powers of Europe would be idle fpectators, content to fuffer the Dutch to engrofs the American colonies or their trade ? And what figure would the Dutch probably make in the unequal conteft ? Their fword has been long fince fheathed in commerce. Thofe of you that have vifited Surinam, and feen a Dutch governor difpenfing at difcretion his own opinions for law, would not fuddenly exchange the Englifh for Dutch government.

I will fubjoin fome obfervations from the Farmer's letters : ' When the appeal is made to the fword, highly pro-

‘ probable it is, that the punishment will exceed the offence,
‘ and the calamities attending on war out-weigh those
‘ preceding it. These considerations of justice and pru-
‘ dence, will always have great influence with good and
‘ wise men. To these reflections it remains to be added,
‘ and ought for ever to be remembered, that resistance, in
‘ the case of the colonies against their mother-country, is
‘ extremely different from the resistance of a people against
‘ their Prince: A nation may change their King or race of
‘ Kings, and, retaining their ancient form of government, be
‘ gainers by changing. Thus Great-Britain, under the il-
‘ lustrious house of Brunswick, a house that seems to
‘ flourish for the happiness of mankind, has found a feli-
‘ city unknown in the reigns of the Stuarts. But if once
‘ we are separated from our mother-country, what new
‘ form of government shall we adopt, or where shall we
‘ find another Britain to supply our loss ? Torn from the
‘ body to which we are united by religion, laws, affection,
‘ relation, language and commerce, we must bleed at every
‘ vein. IN TRUTH, THE PROSPERITY OF THESE PROVINCES
‘ IS FOUNDED IN THEIR DEPENDANCE ON GREAT-BRITAIN. ’

MASSACHUSETTENSIS.

January 30, 1775.

LETTER IX.

To the Inhabitants of the Province of Massachusetts-Bay.

WHEN we reflect upon the constitutional connection
between Great-Britain and the colonies, view the
reciprocation of interest, consider that the welfare of Britain in some measure, and the prosperity of America
wholly, depends upon that connection ; it is astonishing,
indeed almost incredible, that one person should be found
on either side of the Atlantic, so base and destitute of every
sentiment of justice, as to attempt to destroy or weaken
it. If there are none such, in the name of Almighty God,
let me ask ; wherefore is rebellion, that implacable fiend
to society, suffered to rear its ghastly front among us, blast-
ing with haggard look each social joy, and embittering
every hour ?

Re-

Rebellion is the moſt atrocious offence that can be per-
petrated by man, ſave thoſe which are committed more immediately againſt the ſupreme Governor of the univerſe,
who is the avenger of his own cauſe. It diſſolves the ſo-
cial band, annihilates the ſecurity reſulting from law and
government, introduces fraud, violence, rapine, murder,
ſacrilege, and the long train of evils that riot uncontrouled
in a ſtate of nature. Allegiance and protection are reciprocal. The ſubject is bound by the compact to yield
obedience to government, and in return is entitled to protection from it. Thus the poor are protected againſt the
rich, the weak againſt the ſtrong, the individual againſt
the many; and this protection is guaranteed to each member, by the whole community : but when government is
laid proſtrate, a ſtate of war of all againſt all commences;
might overcomes right; innocence itſelf has no ſecurity,
unleſs the individual ſequeſters himſelf from his fellowmen,
inhabits his own cave, and ſeeks his own prey. This
is what is called *a ſtate of nature.* I once thought it
chimerical.

The puniſhment, inflicted upon rebels and traitors in all
ſtates, bears ſome proportion to the aggravated crime.
By our law the puniſhment is, ' That the offender be drawn
' to the gallows, and not be carried or walk ; that he be
' hanged by the neck, and then cut down alive, that his
' entrails be taken out and burned while he is yet alive,
' that his head be cut off, that his body be divided into
' four parts, that his head and quarters be at the King's
' diſpoſal.' The conſequences of attainder are forfeiture
and corruption of blood.

' Forfeiture is twofold, of *real* and of *perſonal* eſtate ; by
' attainder in high treaſon a man forfeits to the King all his
' lands and tenements of inheritance, whether fee ſimple
' or fee tail, and all his rights of entry on lands and tene-
' ments, which he had at the time of the offence committed,
' or at any time afterwards, to be for ever veſted in the
' crown. The forfeiture relates back to the time of the
' treaſon being committed, ſo as to avoid all intermediate
' ſales and incumbrances ; even the dower of the wife is forfeited.

'feited. The natural justice of forfeiture or confiscation
'of property, for treason, is founded in this consideration,
'that he, who has thus violated the fundamental principles
'of government, and broken his part of the original con-
'tract between King and people, hath abandoned his con-
'nections with society, and hath no longer any right to those
'advantages which before belonged to him, purely as a
'member of the community ; among which social advan-
'tages the right of transferring or transmitting property to
'others, is one of the chief. Such forfeitures, moreover,
'whereby his posterity must suffer as well as himself, will
'help to restrain a man, not only by the sense of his duty
'and dread of personal punishment, but also by his passions
'and natural affections ; and will influence every dependent
'and relation he has to keep him from offending.' 4
Black. 374. 375.

It is remarkable however, that this offence, notwithstanding it is of a crimson colour and of the deepest dye, and
its just punishment is not confined to the person of the offender, but beggars all his family, is sometimes committed
by persons who are not conscious of guilt : Sometimes
they are ignorant of the law, and do not foresee the evils
they bring upon society ; at others, they are induced to
think that their cause is founded in the eternal principles
of justice and truth, that they are only making an appeal
to heaven, and may justly expect its decree in their favour.
Doubtless, many of the rebels in the year 1745 were buoyed
up with such sentiments : nevertheless they were cut down
like grass before the scythe of the mower ; the gibbet and
scaffold received those that the sword, wearied with destroying, had spared ; and what loyalist shed one pitying
tear over their graves? They were incorrigible rebels, and
deserved their fate. The community is in less danger
when the disaffected attempt to excite a rebellion against
the *person* of the Prince, than when *government* itself is
the object ; because in the former case the questions are
few, simple, and their solutions obvious, the fatal consequences more apparent, and the loyal people more alert to

K   sup-

suppress it in embryo : whereas, in the latter, a hundred rights of the people, inconsistent with government, and as many grievances, destitute of foundation, the mere creatures of distempered brains, are pourtrayed in the liveliest colours, and serve as bug-bears to affright from their duty, or as decoys to allure the ignorant, the credulous and the unwary to their destruction. Their suspicions are drowned in the perpetual roar for liberty and country ; and even the professions of allegiance to the person of the King, are improved as means to subvert his government.

In mentioning high-treason in the course of these papers, I may not always have expressed myself with the precision of the lawyers ; they have a language peculiar to themselves : I have examined their books, and beg leave to lay before you some further extracts which deserve your attention : ' To levy war against the King, was high-treason by the common law, 3 inst. 9. This is also declared to be high-treason by the stat. of 25 Ed. 3. c. 2. and by the law of this province, 8 W. 3. c. 5.—Assembling in warlike array, against a statute, is levying war against the King, 1 Hale 133. So, to destroy any trade generally, 146. riding with banners displayed, or forming into companies—or being furnished with military officers—or armed with military weapons, as swords, guns, &c. any one of these circumstances carries the *speciem belli*, and will support an indictment for high-treason in levying war, 150 —An insurrection to raise the price of servants wages was held to be an overt act of this species of treason, because this was done *in defiance of the statute* of labourers, it was done in defiance of the *King's authority*, 5 Bac. 117. cites 3 inst.10. —Every assembling of a number of men in a warlike manner, with a design to redress any *public grievance*, is likewise an overt act of this species of treason, because this, being an attempt to do that by *private authority*, which only ought to be done by the King's authority, is an invasion of the prerogative, 5 Bac. 117. cites 3 inst. 9. Ha. p. c.14. Kel. 71. Sid. 358. 1 Hawk. 37.—Every assembling of a number of men in a *warlike* manner, with an intention to reform the government, or the law, is an overt act of this

species

fpecies of treafon, 5 Bac. 117. cites 3 inft. 9. 10. Poph.
122 Kel. 76. 7. 1 Hawk, 37.—*Levying war* may be by
taking arms, not only to dethrone the King, but under
pretence to reform religion, or the *laws*, or to remove evil
counfellors, or other grievances, whether *real* or *pretend-
ed*, 4 Black. 81. Fofter 211.—If any levy war to expel
ftrangers,—to deliver men out of prifon,—to remove counfellors,—*or againft any ftatute*,—or to any other end, pre-
tending reformation of their own heads, without warrant ;
this is levying war againft the King, becaufe they take upon
them royal authority which is againft the King, 3 inft. 9.
—If three, four or more, rife to pull down *an inclofure*,
this is a riot ; but if they had rifen of purpofe to alter religion eftablifhed within the realm, or laws, or to go from
town to town generally, and caft down inclofures, this is
a levying of war (though there be no great number of con-
fpirators) within the perview of this ftatute ; becaufe the
pretence is *public* and *general*, and not *private* in particular,
3 inft. 9. Fofter 211.—If any with ftrength and weapons,
invafive and defenfive, do hold and defend a caftle or fort
againft the King and his power, this is levying of war
againft the King, 3 inft. 10. Fofter 219. 1 Hale 146.296.
—It was refolved by all the judges of England in the reign
of Henry the 8th, that an infurrection againft the ftatute
of labourers, for the inhancing of falaries and wages, was
a levying of war againft the King, becaufe it was generally againft the *King's law*, and the offenders took upon
them the reformation thereof, which fubjects by gathering
of power, ought not to do, 3 inft. 10.—All rifings in order to effect innovations of a *public* and *general* concern,
by an armed force, are, in conftruction of law, high-treafon within the claufe of levying war.— For though they are
not levelled at the perfon of the King, they are againft his
royal Majefty. And befides, they have a direct tendency
to diffolve all the bonds of fociety, and to deftroy all property, and all government too, by numbers and an armed
force, Fofter 211. In Benftead's cafe, Cro. car. 593. At a con-
ference of all the juftices and barons, it was refolved, that
going to Lambeth houfe, in warlike manner, to furprife
the

the Archbifhop, who was a privy-counfellor. (it being with drums and a multitude) to the number of three hundred perfons, was treafon ; upon which Fofter (page 212) ob-ferves, that if it did appear by the libel (which he fays was previoufly pofted up at the Exchange, exhorting the appren-tices to rife and fack the Bifhop's houfe, upon the Monday following) or by the cry of the rabble, at Lambeth houfe, that the attempt was made on account of meafures *the King had taken, or was then taking at the inftigation, as they ima-gined, of the Archbifhop,* and that the rabble had *deliberately,* and upon a *public invitation,* attempted by *numbers* and open force, to take a *fevere revenge* upon the *privy counfellor* for the meafures the Sovereign had taken or was purfuing ; the *grounds and reafons* of the refolution would be fufficiently explained, without taking that *little* circumftance of the *drum* into the cafe :—And he delivers it as his opinion (page 208) that no great ftrefs can be laid on that diftinction taken by Ld. C. J. Hale, between an infurrection with, and one without, the appearance of an army formed under lead-ers and provided with military weapons, and with drums, colours, &c. and fays, the *want* of thefe circumftances weighed nothing with the court in the cafes of Damaree and Purchafe, but that it was fupplied by the *number* of the infurgents : That they were provided with axes, crows and fuch like tools, *furor arma miniftrat* ; and adds (page 208) the true criterion in all thefe cafes, is, *quo animo,* did the parties affemble, whether on account of fome *private* quarrel, or (page 211) to effect innovations of a *public* and *general* concern, by an armed force. Upon the cafe of Da-maree and Purchafe (reported 8 ftat. in. 218. to 285.) Judge Fofter obferves (page 215) that ' fince the meeting-' houfes of proteftant diffenters are, by the *toleration act,* ' taken under *protection* of the *law,* the infurrection in ' the prefent cafe (being to pull down all diffenting pro-' teftant meeting-houfes) was to be confidered as a public ' declaration of the rabble *againft that act,* and an attempt ' to render it *ineffectual* by *numbers* and open force.'

If there be a confpiracy to levy war, and afterwards war is levied ; the confpiracy is, in every one of the confpitators, an overt act of this species of treason, for there can be no acceſſary in high-treaſon, 5 Bac. 115. cites 3 inſt. 9. 10. 138 Hales P. C. 14. Kel. 19. 1 Hawk. 38.——A compaſſing or conſpiracy to levy war is no treaſon, for there muſt be a levying of war *in facto*. But if many conſpire to levy war, and ſome of them do levy the ſame according to the conſpiracy; this is high-treaſon in all, for in treaſon all are principals, and war is levied, 3 inſt. 9. Foſter 213.

The *painful* taſk of applying the above rules of law to the ſeveral tranſactions that we have been eye-witneſſes to, will never be mine. Let me however intreat you to make the application in your own minds; and thoſe of you that have continued hitherto " faithful among the faithleſs", Abdiel like, to perſevere in your integrity: and thoſe of you that have already been enſnared by the accurſed wiles of deſigning men, I would exhort to caſt yourſelves immediately upon that mercy, ſo conſpicuous through the Britiſh conſtitution, and which is the brighteſt jewel in the imperial diadem.

MASSACHUSETTENSIS.

February 6, 1775.

L E T T E R   X.

To the Inhabitants of the Province of Maſſachuſetts-Bay.

I Offered to your conſideration, laſt week, a few extracts from the law-books, to enable thoſe, that have been but little converſant with the law of the land, to form a judgment, and determine for themſelves, whether any have been ſo far beguiled and ſeduced from their allegiance, as to commit the moſt aggravated offence againſt ſociety,—high-treaſon. The whigs reply, riots and inſurrections are frequent in England, the land from which we ſprang; we are bone of their bone, and fleſh of their fleſh:—Granted; but at the ſame time be it remembered, that in England the executive power is commonly able and willing to ſuppreſs inſurrections, the judiciary to diſtribute impartial juſtice, and the legiſlative to aid and ſtrengthen the two former if neceſſary; and whenever theſe have proved ineffectual to allay inteſtine commotions, war, with its concomitant hor-

horrors, have paffed through the land, marking their rout with blood : The bigger part of Britain has at fome period or other, within the reach of hiftory, been forfeited to the crown, by the rebellion of its proprietors.

Let us now take a view of American grievances, and try, by the fure touchftone of reafon and the conftitution, whether there be any act or acts, on the part of the King or parliament, that will juftify the whigs even in *foro confcientiæ*, in thus forcibly oppofing their government. Will the alteration of the mode of appointing one branch of our provincial legiflature furnifh fo much as an excufe for it, confidering that our politicians, by their intrigues and machinations, had rendered the affembly incapable of anfwering the purpofe of government, which is protection, and our charter was become as inefficacious as an old ballad ? Or can a plea of juftification be founded on the parliament's giving us an exact tranfcript of Englifh laws for returning jurors, when our own were infufficient to afford compenfation to the injured, to fupprefs feditions, or even to reftrain rebellion ? It has been heretofore obferved, that each member of the community is entitled to protection ; for this he pays taxes, for this he relinquifhes his natural right of revenging injuries and redreffing wrongs, and for this the fword of juftice is placed in the hands of the magiftrate. It is notorious that the whigs had ufurped the power of the province in a great meafure, and exercifed it by revenging themfelves on their opponents, or in compelling them to inlift under their banners. Recollect the frequency of mobs and riots, the invafions and demolitions of dwelling-houfes and other property, the perfonal abufe and frequent neceffity of perfons abandoning their habitations, the taking fanctuary on board men of war, or at the caftle, *previous* to the regulating bill. Confider that thefe fufferers were loyal fubjects, violators of no law, that many of them were crown officers, and were thus perfecuted for no other offence than that of executing the King's law. Confider, further, that if any of the fufferers fought redrefs in a court of law, he had the whole whig intereft to combat : they gathered like a cloud and hovered
like

like harpies round the feat of juftice, until the fuitor was either condemned to pay cofts to his antagonift, or recovered fo fmall damages, as that they were fwallowed up in his own. Confider further, that thefe riots were not the accidental or fpontaneous rifings of the populace, but the refult of the deliberations and mature councils of the whigs, and were fometimes headed and led to action by their principals. Confider further, that the general affembly lent no aid to the executive power. Weigh thefe things, my friends, and doubt if you can, whether the act for regulating our government did not flow from the parental tendernefs of the Britifh councils, to enable us to recover from anarchy, without Britain being driven to the neceffity of inflicting punifhment, which is her ftrange work. Having taken this curfory view of the convulfed ftate of the province, let us advert to our charter-form of government, and we fhall find its diftributions of power to have been fo prepofterous as to render it next to impoffible for the province to recover by its own ftrength. The council was elective annually by the houfe, liable to the negative of the chair; and the chair was reftrained from acting even in the executive department, without the concurrence of the board. The political ftruggle is often between the governor and the houfe; and it is a maxim with politicians, that he that is not for us is againft us: Accordingly, when party runs high, if a councillor adhered to the governor, the houfe refufed to elect him the next year; if he adhered to the houfe, the governor negatived him; if he trimmed his bark, fo as to fteer a middle courfe between Scylla and Charybdis, he was in danger of fuffering more by the neglect of both parties, than of being wrecked but on one.

In moderate times this province has been happy under our charter-form of government; but, when the political ftorm arofe, its original defect became apparent: We have fometimes feen half a dozen fail of tory navigation unable, on an election day, to pafs the bar formed by the flux and reflux of the tides at the entrance of the harbour, and as many whiggifh ones ftranded the next morning on Governor's Ifland. The whigs took the lead in this game; and

there-

therefore I think the blame ought to reft upon them, though the tables were turned upon them in the fequel. A flender acquaintance with human nature will inform us, and experienec has evinced, that a body of men, thus conftituted, are not to be depended upon to act that vigorous, intrepid and decifive part, which the emergency of the late times required, and which might have proved the falvation of the province. In fhort, the board, which was intended to· moderate between the governor and the houfe, or perhaps rather to fupport the former, was incapable of doing either by its original conftitution. By the regulating act the members of the board are appointed by the King in council, and are not liable even to the fufpenfion of the governor; their commiffions are *durante bene placito*, and they are therefore far from independence. The infant ftate of the colonies does not admit of a peerage, nor perhaps of any third branch of legiflature wholly independent. In moft of the colonies the council is appointed by *mandamus*, and the members are moreover liable to be fufpended by the governor; by which means they are more dependent than thofe appointed according to the regulating act, but no inconvenience arifes from that mode of appointment. Long experience has evinced its utility. By this ftatute, extraordinary powers are devolved upon the chair, to enable the governor to maintain his authority, and to oppofe with vigour the daring fpirit of independence, fo manifeft in the whigs. Town-meetings are reftrained to prevent their paffing traiterous refolves. Had thefe, and many other innovations contained in this act, been made in moderate times, when due reverence was yielded to the magiftrate, and obedience to the law, they might have been called grievances; but we have no reafon to think, that, had the fituation of the province been fuch, this ftatute would ever have had an exiftence—nor have we any reafon to doubt, but that it will be repealed, in whole or in part, fhould our prefent form of government be found by experience to be productive of rapine or oppreffion. It is impoffible, that the King, lords or commons could have any finifter views in regulating the government of this province. Sometimes we

we are told that charters are facred : However facred, they
are forfeited through negligence or *abuſe* of their franchiſes,
in which caſes the law judges, that the body politic has
broken the condition upon which it was incorporated.

There are many inſtances of the negligence and abuſe
which work the forfeiture of charters delineated in law books.
They alſo tell us, that all charters may be vacated by act of
parliament. Had the form of our provincial legiſlature
been eſtabliſhed by act of parliament, that act might have
been conſtitutionally and equitably repealed, when it was
found to be incapable of anſwering the end of its inſtitu-
tion. Stronger ſtill is the preſent caſe, where the form of
government was eſtabliſhed by one branch of the legiſlature only, viz. the King, and all three join in the revoca-
tion. This act was however a fatal ſtroke to the ambitious views of our republican patriots. The monarchical part
of the conſtitution was ſo guarded by it, as to be no longer
vulnerable by their ſhafts ; and all their fancied greatneſs
vaniſhed like the baſeleſs fabric of a viſion. Many, who
had been long ſtriving to attain a ſeat at the board, with
their faces thitherward, beheld, with infinite regret, their
competitors advanced to the honors they aſpired to themſelves. Theſe diſappointed, ambitious and envious men
inſtil the poiſon of diſaffection into the minds of the lower
claſſes, and as ſoon as they are properly impregnated, exclaim, *the people* never will ſubmit to it. They now would
urge them into certain ruin, to prevent the execution of
an act of parliament, deſigned and calculated to reſtore
peace and harmony to the province, and to recal that happy ſtate, when year rolled round on year, in a continual
increaſe of our felicity.

The Quebec bill is another capital grievance, becauſe
the Canadians are tolerated in the enjoyment of their religion, which they were entitled to, by an article of capi-
tulation, when they ſubmitted to the Britiſh arms. This
toleration is not an excluſion of the proteſtant religion,
which is eſtabliſhed in every part of the empire, as firmly
as civil polity can eſtabliſh it. It is a ſtrange kind of rea-
ſoning to argue, from the French inhabitants of the con-

L   quered

quered province of Quebec, being tolerated in the enjoyment of the Roman Catholic religion in which they were
educated, and in which alone they repose their hope of eternal salvation, that therefore government intends to deprive
us of the enjoyment of the protestant religion in which alone
we believe; especially as the political interests of Britain depend upon protestant connexions, and the King's being a
protestant himself is an indispensable condition of his wear-
ing the crown. This circumstance, however, served admi-
rably for a fresh stimulus, and was eagerly grasped by the
disaffected of all orders. It added pathos to *pulpit oratory*.
We often see resolves and seditious letters intersperfed with
popery here and there in Italics. If any of the clergy have
endeavoured, from this circumstance, to alarm their too
credulous audiences, with an apprehension that their religious privileges were in danger, thereby to excite them to
take up arms; we must lament the depravity of the best of
men: but human nature stands appalled when we reflect
upon the aggravated guilt of *prostituting our holy religion
to the accursed purposes of treason and rebellion*. As to
our lay politicians, I have long since ceased to wonder at
any thing in them; but it may be observed, that there is no
surer mark of a bad cause than for its advocates to recur
to such pitiful shifts to support it. This instance plainly
indicates, that their sole dependence is in preventing the
passions subsiding, and cool reason resuming its seat. It is
a mark of their shrewdness however, for whenever reason
shall resume its seat, the political cheat will be detected,
stand confest in its native turpitude, and the political knave
be branded with marks of infamy, adequate, if possible, to
the enormity of his crimes.

MASSACHUSETTENSIS.

February 13, 1775.

LETTER XI.
To the Inhabitants of the Province of Massachusetts-Bay.

IT would be an endless task to remark minutely upon
each of the fancied grievances, that swarm and cluster,

fill

fill and deform, the American chronicles. An adeptness at
difcovering grievances, has lately been one of the principal recommendations to public notice and popular applaufe.
We have had geniufes felected for that purpofe, called *committees upon grievances*; a fagacious fet they were, and
difcovered a multitude before it was known, that they themfelves were the greateft grievances that the country was in-
fefted with. Tne cafe is fhortly this; the whigs fuppofe
the colonies to be feparate or diftinct ftates: having fixed
this opinion in their minds, they are at no lofs for grievances.
Could I agree with them in their firft principle, I fhould
acquiefce in many of their deductions; for in that cafe every act of parliament extending to the colonies, and every
movement of the crown to carry them into execution,
would be really grievances, however wife and falutary they
might be in themfelves; as they would be exertions of a
power that we were not conftitutionally fubject to, and
would deferve the name of ufurpation and tyranny. But
deprived of this, their corner ftone, the terrible fabric of
grievances vanifhes like caftles raifed by enchantment, and
leaves the wondering fpectator amazed and confounded at
the deception. He fufpects himfelf to have but juft awoke
from fleep, or recovered from a trance, and that the formidable fpectre that had frozen him with horror, was no more
than the creature of a vifion, or the delufion of a dream.

Upon this point, whether the colonies are diftinct ftates
or not, our patriots have rafhly tendered Great Britain an
iffue, againft every principle of law and conftitution, againft
reafon and common prudence. There is no arbiter between
us but the *fword*; and that the decifion of that tribunal
will be againft us, reafon forefees, as plainly as it can difcover any event that lies in the womb of futurity. No perfon, unlefs actuated by ambition, pride, malice, envy, or
a malignant combination of the whole that verges towards
madnefs, and hurries the man away from himfelf, would
wage war upon fuch unequal terms. No honeft man would
engage himfelf, much lefs plunge his country into the calamities of a war upon equal terms, without firft fettling
with his confcience, in the retired moments of reflection,

the

the important queſtion reſpecting the juſtice of his cauſe.
To do this, we muſt hear and weigh every thing that is
fairly adduced, on either ſide of the queſtion, with equal
attention and care : *a diſpoſition to drink in with avidity,
what favours our hypotheſis, and to reject with diſguſt whatever contravenes, is an infallible mark of a narrow, ſelfiſh
mind.* In matters of ſmall moment ſuch obſtinacy is weak-
neſs and folly, in important ones, fatal madneſs. There
are many among us, who have devoted themſelves to the
ſlaviſh dominion of prejudice; indeed the more liberal have
ſeldom had an opportunity of bringing the queſtion to a
fair examination. The eloquence of the bar, the pulpit, and
the ſenate, the charms or poetry, the expreſſions of painting,
ſculpture and ſtatuary, have conſpired to fix and rivet ideas
of independence upon the mind of the coloniſts. The over-
whelming torrent, ſupplied from ſo many fountains, rolled
on with increaſing rapidity and violence, till it became ſuperior to all reſtraint. It was the reign of paſſion; the ſmall,
ſtill voice of reaſon was refuſed audience. I have obſerved
that the preſs was heretofore open to but one ſide of the
queſtion, which has given offence to a writer in Edes and
Gill's paper, under the ſignature of Novanglus, to whom
I have many things to ſay. I would at preſent aſk him, if
the convention of committees for the county of Worceſter
in recommending to the inhabitants of that county not to
take news papers, publiſhed by two of the printers in this
town, and two at New-York, have not affected to be licenſers of the preſs? And whether, by proſcribing theſe
printers, and endeavouring to deprive them of a livelihood,
they have not manifeſted an illiberal, bigotted, arbitrary,
malevolent diſpoſition? And whether, by thus attempting
to deſtroy the liberty of the preſs, they have not betrayed
a conſciouſneſs of the *badneſs of their cauſe?*

Our warriors tell us, that the parliament ſhall be permitted to legiſlate for the purpoſes of regulating trade, but
the parliament hath moſt unrighteouſly aſſerted, that it
" had, hath, and of right ought to have, full power and
" authority to make laws and ſtatutes of ſufficient force
" and validity to bind the colonies in all caſes whatſoever;"
that

that this claim, being without any qualification or reftriction, is an innovation, and inconfiftent with liberty. Let us candidly enquire into thefe three obfervations, upon the ftatute declaratory of the authority of parliament. As to its univerfality, it is true there are no exceptions expreffed; but there is no general rule without exceptions, expreffed or implied.

The implied ones in this cafe are obvious. It is evident that the intent and meaning of this act, was to affert the fupremacy of parliament in the colonies, that is, that its conftitutional authority to make laws and ftatutes binding upon the colonies, is, and ever had been, as ample, as it is to make laws binding upon the realm. No one that reads the declaratory ftatute, not even prejudice itfelf, can fuppofe that the parliament meant to affert thereby a right or power to deprive the colonifts of their lives, to enflave them, or to make any law refpecting the colonies, that would not be conftitutional, were it made refpecting Great Britain. By an act of parliament paffed in the year 1650, it was declared concerning the colonies and plantations in America, that they had " ever fince the planting thereof been and " ought to be fubject to fuch laws, orders and regulations, " as are or fhall be made by the parliament of England." This declaration, though differing in expreffion, is the fame in fubftance with the other. Our Houfe of reprefentatives, in their difpute with Governor Hutchinfon, concerning the fupremacy of parliament, fay, " It is difficult, if poffible, " to draw a line of diftinction between the univerfal au- " thority of parliament over the colonies and no authority " at all."

The declaratory ftatute was intended more efpecially to affert the right of parliament, to make laws and ftatutes for raifing a revenue in America, left the repeal of the ftamp-act might be urged as a difclaimer of the right. Let us now enquire, whether a power to raife a revenue be not the inherent, unalienable right of the fupreme legiflature of every well-regulated ftate, where the hereditary revenue of the crown, or eftablifhed revenues of the ftate are infufficient of themfelves ; and whether that power be not necef-

farily

farily coëxtenfive with the power of legiflation, or rather neceffarily implied in it.

The end or defign of government, as has been already obferved, is the fecurity of the people from internal vio- lence and rapacity, and from foreign invafion. The fu- preme power of a ftate muft neceffarily be fo extenfive and ample as to anfwer thofe purpofes ; otherwife it is confti- tuted in vain, and degenerates into empty parade and mere oftentatatious pageantry. Thefe purpofes cannot be an- fwered, without a power to raife a revenue ; for without it neither the laws can be executed nor the ftate defended. This revenue ought, in national concerns, to be apportioned throughout the whole empire according to the abilities of the feveral parts ; as the claim of each to protection is equal : a refufal to yield the former is as unjuft as the withholding the latter. Were any part of an empire ex- empt from contributing their proportionable part of the revenue neceffary for the whole, fuch exemption would be manifeft injuftice to the reft of the empire ; as it muft of courfe bear more than its proportion of the public burden, and it would amount to an additional tax. If the propor- tion of each part was to be determined only by itfelf in a feparate legiflature ; it would not only involve it in the ab- furdity of *imperium in imperio*, but the perpetual contention arifing from the predominant principle of felf-intereft in each, without having any common arbiter between them, would render the disjointed, difcordant, torn and difmem- bered ftate incapable of collecting or conducting its force and energy, for the prefervation of the whole, as emergen- cies might require. A government thus conftituted would contain the feeds of diffolution in its firft principles, and muft foon deftroy itfelf.

I have already fhewn that, by your firft charter, this pro- vince was to be fubject to taxation after the lapfe of twenty- one years, and that the authority of parliament to impofe fuch taxes was claimed fo early as the year 1642.

In the patent for Pennfylvania, which is now in force, there is this claufe, " And further our pleafure is, and by " thefe prefents, for us, &c. we do covenant and agree to

" and

" and with the faid William Penn, &c. that we, &c. fhall
" at no time hereafter fet or make, or caufe to be fet, any
" impofition, cuftom or other taxation, or rate or contri-
" bution whatfoever, in and upon the dwellers and inhabi-
" tants of the aforefaid province, for their lands, tenements,
" goods or chattels within the faid province, or in and upon
" any goods or merchandife within the faid province, to be
" laden or unladen within the ports or harbours of the faid
" province, *unlefs* the fame be with the confent of the pro-
" prietors, chief governor or affembly, or by *act of parlia-*
" *ment.*"

Thefe are ftubborn facts : they are incapable of being
winked out of exiftence, how much foever we may be difpofed to fhut our eyes upon them. They prove that the
claim of a right to raife a revenue in the colonies, exclufive
of the grants of their own affemblies, is coëval with the
colonies themfelves. I fhall next fhew, that there has been
an actual, uninterrupted exercife of that right by the parliament, time immemorial.

MASSACHUSETTENSIS.

February 20, 1775.

L E T T E R   XII.

To the Inhabitants of the Province of Maffachufetts-Bay.

BY an act of parliament, made in the twenty-fifth year
of the reign of Charles the fecond, duties are laid upon goods and merchandife of various kinds, exported from
the colonies to foreign countries, or carried from one colony to another, payable on exportation. I will recite a part
of it ; viz. ' For fo much of the faid commodities as fhall
' be laden and put on board fuch fhip or veffel, that is to
' fay, for fugar white the hundred weight, five fhillings ;
' and brown and Mufcovados the hundred weight, one fhil-
' ling and fixpence ; tobacco the pound, one penny ; cot-
' ton wool the pound, one half-penny ; for indigo two
' pence ; ginger the hundred weight, one fhilling ; log-
' wood the hundred weight, five pounds ; fuftic and all
' other dying wood the hundred weight, fix pence ; cocoa
' the

' the pound, one penny, to be *levied, collected, and paid* at
' fuch places and to fuch collectors and other officers, as
' *fhall be appointed* in the refpective plantations, to collect,
' levy and receive the fame before the landing thereof, and
' under fuch penalties both to the officers and upon the
' goods, as for non-payment of, or *defrauding his majefty of
' his cuftoms in England.* And for the better *collecting of the
' feveral rates and duties impofed by this act,* be it enacted, that
' this whole bufinefs fhall be ordered and managed, and the
' feveral duties hereby impofed fhall be caufed *to be levied
' by the commiffioners of the cuftoms in England,* by and under
' the authority of the lord treafurer of England, or com-
' miffioners of the treafury.'

It is apparent, from the reafoning of this ftatute, that
thefe duties were impofed for the fole purpofe of revenue.
There has lately been a moft ingenious play upon the words
and expreffions, *tax, revenue, purpofe of raifing a revenue,
fole purpofe of raifing a revenue, exprefs purpofe of raifing
a revenue*; as though their being inferted in or left
out of a ftatute, would make any effential difference
in the ftatute. This is mere playing with words; for
if, from the whole tenor of the act, it is evident, that
the intent of the legiflature was to tax, rather than to regulate the trade, by impofing duties on goods and merchandife; it is to all intents and purpofes an inftance of taxation,
be the form of words, in which the ftatute is conceived,
what it will. That fuch was the intent of the legiflature,
in this inftance, any one that will take the pains to read it
will be convinced. There have been divers alterations
made in this by fubfequent ftatutes; but fome of the above
taxes remain, and are collected and paid in the colonies to
this day. By an act of the 7th and 8th of William and Mary
it is enacted, ' that every feaman whatfoever that fhall ferve
' his majefty, or any other perfon whatever in any of his ma-
' jefty's fhips or veffels whatfoever, belonging or to belong
' to any fubjects of England, or any other his majefty's do-
' minions, fhall allow, and there fhall be paid out of the
' wages of every fuch feaman, to grow due for fuch his fer-
' vice, fix pence per annum for the better fupport of the
' faid hofpital, and to augment the *revenue* thereof.' This

tax

tax was impofed in the reign of King William the third, of bleffed memory, and is ftill levied in the colonies. It would require a volume to recite or minutely remark upon all the revenue acts that relate to America. We find them in many reigns, impofing new duties, taking off, or reducing, old ones, and making provifion for their collection, or new appropriations of them. By an act of the 7th and 8th of William and Mary, entitled ' an act for preventing frauds ' and regulating abufes in the plantations,' all former acts refpecting the plantations are renewed, and all fhips and veffels, coming into any port here, are liable to the fame regulations and reftrictions as fhips in the ports in England are liable to; and it enacts ' *That the officers for collecting* ' *and managing his majefty's revenue, and infpecting the plan-* ' *tation trade in many of the faid plantations,* fhall have the ' fame powers and authority for vifiting and fearching of ' fhips and taking their entries, and for feizing, or fecuring, ' or bringing on fhore, any of the goods prohibited to be ' imported or exported into or out of any of the faid colo- ' nies and plantations, *or for which any duties are payable* ' *or ought to be paid by any of the before mentioned acts, as are* ' *provided for the officers of the cuftoms in England.*' The act of the 9th of Queen Anne, for eftablifhing a poft-office, gives this reafon for its eftablifhment, and for laying taxes thereby impofed on the carriage of letters in Great-Britain and Ireland, the colonies and plantations in North-America and the Weft-Indies, and all other his majefty's dominions and territories, ' that the bufinefs may be ' done in fuch manner as may be moft beneficial to the ' people of thefe kingdoms, and her majefty may be fup- ' plied, and the revenue arifing by the faid office, better ' improved, fettled and fecured to her majefty, her heirs and ' fucceffors.' The celebrated patriot, Dr. Franklin, was till lately one of the principal collectors of it. The merit in putting the poft-office in America upon fuch a footing as to yield a large revenue to the crown, is principally af- cribed to him by the whigs. I would not wifh to detract from the real merit of that gentleman; but, had a tory been half fo affiduous in increafing the American revenue, No-

M   vanglus

vanglus would have wrote parricide at the end of his name. By an act of the sixth of George the second, a duty is laid on all foreign rum, melasses, syrups, sugars and paneles, to be *raised, levied, collected and paid unto and for the use of his majesty, his heirs and successors.* The preamble of an act of the fourth of his present majesty declares, that ' *it is just* ' *and necessary that a revenue in America for defraying the ex-* ' *pences of defending, protecting and securing the same,*' &c. by which act duties are laid upon foreign sugars, coffee, Madeira wine; upon Portugal, Spanish and all other wine (except French wine) imported from Great-Britain; upon silks, bengals, stuffs, callico, linen cloth, cambric and lawn, imported from particular places.

Thus, my friends, it is evident, that the parliament has been in the actual, uninterrupted use and exercise of the right claimed by them, to raise a revenue in America, from a period more remote than the grant of the present charter, to this day. These revenue acts have never been called unconstitutional till very lately. Both whigs and tories acknowledged them to be constitutional. In 1764 Governor Bernard wrote and transmitted to his friends his polity alluded to, and in part received by Novanglus, wherein he asserts the right or authority of parliament to tax the colonies. Mr. Otis, whose patriotism, sound policy, profound learning, integrity and honour, is mentioned in strong terms by Novanglus, in the self-same year, in a pamphlet which he publishes to the whole world, asserts the right or authority of parliament to tax the colonies, as roundly as ever Governor Bernard did, which I shall have occasion to take an extract from hereafter. Mr. Otis was at that time the most popular man in the province, and continued his popularity many years afterwards.

Is it not a most astonishing instance of caprice, or infatuation, that a province, torn from its foundations, should be precipitating itself into a war with Great-Britain, because the British parliament asserts its right of raising a revenue in America; inasmuch as the claim of that right is as antient as the colonies themselves, and there is at present no grievous exercise of it? The parliament's refusing to repeal the

tea

tea act is the oftenfible foundation of our quarrel. If we afk the whigs, whether the pitiful three-penny duty upon a luxurious, unwholefome, foreign commodity, gives juft occafion for the oppofition; they tell us, it is the precedent they are contending about, infinuating that it is an innovation. But this ground is not tenable; for a total repeal of the tea-act would not ferve us upon the fcore of precedents. They are numerous without this. The whigs have been extremely partial refpecting tea. Poor tea has been made the fhibboleth of party; while melaffes, wine, coffee, indigo, &c. &c. have been unmolefted. A perfon that drinks New-England rum, diftilled from melaffes fubject to a like duty, is equally deferving of a coat of tar and feathers with him that drinks tea. A coffee drinker is as culpable as either, viewed in a political light. But, fay our patriots, if the Britifh parliament may take a penny from us without our confent, they may a pound, and fo on, till they have filched away all our property. This inceffant incantation operates like a fpell or a charm, and checks the efforts of loyalty in many an honeft breaft. Let us give it its full weight: Do they mean that if the parliament has a right to raife a revenue of one penny on the colonies, that they muft therefore have a *right* to wreft from us all our property? If this be their meaning, I deny their deduction; for the fupreme legiflature can have no right to tax any part of the empire to a greater amount, than its juft and equitable proportion of the neceffary national expence. This is a line drawn by the conftitution itfelf. Do they mean, that, if we admit that the parliament may conftitutionally raife one penny upon us for the purpofes of revenue, they will probably proceed from light to heavy taxes, till their impofitions become grievous and intolerable? This amounts to no more than a denial of the right, *left* it fhould be abufed. But an argument drawn from the actual abufe of a power, will not conclude to the illegality of fuch power; much lefs will an argument drawn from the capability of its being abufed. If it would, we might readily argue away all power that man is intrufted with. I will admit, that a power of taxation is more liable

to

to abufe than legiflation feparately confidered; and it would give me pleafure to fee fome other line drawn, fome other barrier erected, than what the conftitution has already done, if it be poffible, whereby the conftitutional authority of the fupreme legiflature might be preferved intire, and America be guaranteed in every right and exemption, confiftent with her fubordination and dependence. But this can only be done by *parliament*. I repeat, I am no advocate for a land-tax, or any other kind of internal tax, nor do I think we were in any danger of them ; I have not been able to difcover one fymptom of any fuch intention in the parliament, fince the repeal of the ftamp-act. Indeed the principal fpeakers of the majority, that repealed the ftamp-act, drew the line for us, between internal and external taxation; and I think we ought, in honour, juftice, and good policy, to have acquiefced therein, at leaft till there was fome burdenfome exercife of taxation. For there is but little danger from the latter, that is, from duties laid upon trade; as any grievous reftriction or impofition on American trade, would be fenfibly felt by the Britifh ; and I think, with Dr. Franklin, that ' they (the Britifh nation) have a ' natural and equitable right to fome toll or duty upon mer' chandifes carried through that part of their dominions, ' viz. the American feas, towards defraying the expence ' they are at in fhips to maintain the fafety of that carriage.' Thefe were his words in his examination at the bar of the houfe, in 1765. *Sed tempora mutantur, et nos mutamur in illis.* Before we appeal to heaven for the juftice of our cau e, we ought to determine, with ourfelves, fome other queftions, whether America is not obliged in equity to contribute fomething toward the national defence : Whether the prefent American revenue amounts to our proportion : And whether we can, with any tolerable grace, accufe Great-Britain of *injuftice* in impofing the late duties, when our Affemblies were previoufly called upon, and refufed to make any provifion for themfelves. Thefe, with feveral imaginary grievances, not yet particularly remarked upon, I fhall confider in reviewing the publications of Novanglus ; a performance, which, though not deftitute of ingenuity, I read

with

with a mixture of grief and indignation, as it feems to be calculated to blow up every fpark of animofity, and to kindle fuch a flame, as muft inevitably confume a great part of this once happy province, before it can be extinguifhed.

MASSACHUSETTENSIS.

February 27, 1775.

LETTER XIII.

To the Inhabitants of the Province of Maffachufetts-Bay.

NOVANGLUS and all others have an indifputable right to publifh their fentiments and opinions to the world, provided they conform to truth, decency and the municipal laws of the fociety of which they are members. He has wrote with a profeffed defign of expofing the errors and fophiftry, which he fuppofes are frequent in my publications : His defign is fo far laudable ; and I intend to correct them wherever he convinces me there is an inftance of either. I have no objection to the minuteft difquifition : contradiction and difputation, like the collifion of flint and fteel, often ftrike out new light. The bare opinions of either of us, accompanied by the grounds and reafons upon which they were formed, muft be confidered only as propofitions made to the reader for him to adopt or reject, as his own reafon may judge, or feelings dictate. A large proportion of the labours of Novanglus confift in denials of my allegations in matters of fuch public notoriety, as that no reply is neceffary : He has alledged many things deftitute of foundation. Thofe that affect the main object of our purfuit but remotely, if at all, I fhall pafs by without particular remark ; others, of a more interefting nature, I fhall review minutely. After fome general obfervations upon Maffachufettenfis, he flides into a moft virulent attack upon particular perfons, by names, with fuch incomparable eafe, that fhews him to be a great proficient in the modern art of detraction and calumny. He accufes the late Governor Shirley, Governor Hutchinfon, the late Lieutenant Governor Oliver, the late Judge Ruffell, Mr Paxton, and Brigadier Ruggles, of a confpiracy to enflave their country. The

charge

charge is high coloured : if it be juft, they merit the epi-
thets, dealt about fo indifcriminately, of enemies to their
country ; if it be groundlefs, Novanglus has acted the part
of an affaffin, in thus attempting to deftroy the reputation
of the living, and of fomething worfe than an affaffin, in
entering thofe hallowed manfions, where the wicked commonly ceafe from troubling and the weary are at reft, to
difturb the repofe of the dead. That the charge is groundlefs refpecting Governor Bernard, Governor Hutchinfon,
and the late Lieutenant Governor, I dare affert ; becaufe
they have been acquitted of it in fuch a manner as every
good citizen muft acquiefce in. Our houfe of reprefentatives, acting as the grand inqueft of the province, prefented
them before the King in council ; and after a full hearing
they were acquitted with honor, and the feveral impeach-
ments difmiffed, as *groundlefs, vexatious* and *fcandalous.*
The accufation of the houfe was fimilar to this of Novanglus ; the court, they chofe to inftitute their fuit in, was of
competent and high jurifdiction, and its decifion final. This
is a fufficient anfwer to the ftate charges made by this writer,
fo far as they refpect the Governors Bernard, Hutchinfon
and Oliver, whom he accufes as principals ; and it is a general rule, that, if the principal be innocent, the acceffary
cannot be guilty. A determination of a conftitutional arbiter ought to feal up the lips of even prejudice itfelf in filence ; otherwife litigation muft be endlefs. This calum-
niator neverthelefs has the effrontery to renew the charge
in a public news-paper, although thereby he arraigns our
moft gracious Sovereign and the lords of the privy council,
as well as the gentlemen he has named. Not content with
wounding the honor of judges, counfellors and governors,
with miffile weapons, darted from an obfcure corner, he
now aims a blow at Majefty itfelf. Any one may accufe,
but accufation unfupported by proof recoils upon the head
of the accufer. It is entertaining enough to confider the
crimes and mifdemeanors alledged, and then examine the
evidence he adduces, ftript of the falfe glare he has thrown
upon it.

The crimes are thefe ; the perfons named by him confpired together to *enflave* their country, in confequence of
a plan

a plan, the outlines of which have been drawn by Sir Edmund Andros and others, and handed down by tradition to the prefent times. He tells us that Governor Shirley, in 1754, communicated the profound fecret, the great defign of taxing the colonies by act of parliament, to the fagacious gentleman, eminent philofopher, and diftinguifhed patriot, Dr. Franklin. The profound fecret is this; after the commencement of hoftilities between the Englifh and French colonies in the laft war, a convention of committees from feveral provinces were called by the King to agree upon fome general plan of defence : The principal difficulty they met with was in divifing means, whereby each colony might be obliged to contribute its proportionable part. General Shirley propofed, *that application fhould be made to parliament to impower the committees of the feveral colonies to tax the whole according to their feveral proportions.* This plan was adopted by the convention, and approved of by the affembly in New-York, who paffed a refolve in thefe words: ‘ That the fcheme propofed by Governor ‘ Shirley, for the defence of the Britifh colonies in North- ‘ America, is well concerted, and that this colony joins ‘ therein.’ This however did not fucceed, and he propofed another, viz. for the parliament to affefs each one’s proportion, and, in cafe of failure to raife it on their part, that it fhould be done by parliament. This is the profound fecret. His affiduity, in endeavouring to have fome effectual plan of general defence eftablifhed, is, by the falfe colouring of this writer, reprefented as an attempt to aggrandize himfelf, family and friends; and that gentleman, under whofe adminiftration the feveral parties in the province were as much united and the whole province rendered as happy as it ever was, for fo long a time together, is called a ‘ crafty, bufy, ambitious, intriguing, enterprizing man.’ This attempt of Governor Shirley, for a parliamentary taxation, is however a circumftance ftrongly militating with this writer’s hypothefis ; for the approbation fhewn to the Governor’s propofal by the convention, which confifted of perfons from the feveral colonies, not inferior in point of difcernment, integrity, knowledge or patriotifm to the

mem-

members of our late *grand Congress*, and the vote of the
New-York affembly, furnifh pretty ftrong evidence that
the authority of parliament, even in point of taxation,
was not doubted in that day.—Even Dr. Franklin, in the
letter alluded to, does not deny the *right*.—His objections
go to the *inexpediency* of the meafure.—He fuppofes it
would create uneafinefs in the minds of the colonifts,
fhould they be thus taxed; unlefs they were previoufly allowed to fend reprefentatives to parliament. If Dr.
Franklin really fuppofes, that the Parliament has no conftitutional right to raife a revenue in America, I muft confefs myfelf at a lofs to reconcile his conduct in accepting
the office of poft-mafter, and his affiduity in increafing
the revenue in that department, to the patriotifm predi-
cated of him by Novanglus, efpecially as this unfortunately
happens to be an internal tax. This writer tells us, that
the plan was interrupted by the war, and afterwards by
Governor Pownall's adminiftration. That Meffieurs Hutchinfon and Oliver, ftung with envy at Governor Pownall's
favourites, propagated flanders refpecting him to render
him uneafy in his feat. My anfwer is this, that he that
publifhes fuch falfhoods as thefe in a public news-paper,
with an air of ferioufnefs, infults the underftanding of the
public, more than he injures the individuals he defames.
In the next place we are told, that Governor Bernard was
the proper man for this purpofe; and he was employed by
the junto to fuggeft to the miniftry the project of taxing
the colonies by act of parliament. Sometimes Governor
Bernard is the arch enemy of America, the fource of all
our troubles; now, only a tool in the hands of others. I
wifh Novanglus's memory had ferved him better; his tale
might have been confiftent with itfelf, however contrary
to truth. After making thefe affertions with equal gra-
vity and affurance, he tells, us he does not advance this
without evidence. I had been looking out for evidence a
long time, and was all attention when it was promifed;
but my difappointment was equal to the expectation he
had raifed, when I found the evidence amounted to nothing
more than Governor Bernard's letters and principles of
law

law and polity, wherein he afferts the fupremacy of parliament over the colonies both as to legiflation and taxation.
Where this writer got his logic, I do not know. Reduced
to a fyllogifm, his argument ftands thus : Governor Bernard, in 1764, wrote and tranfmitted to England certain
letters and principles of law and polity, wherein he afferts
the right of parliament to tax the colonies. Meffieurs
Hutchinfon and Oliver were in unifon with him in all his
meafures : therefore, Meffieurs Hutchinfon and Oliver employed Governor Bernard to fuggeft to the miniftry the
projeft of taxing the colonies by aft of parliament. The
letters and principles are the whole of the evidence ; and
this is all the appearance of argument contained in his
publication. Let us examine the premifes. That Governor Bernard afferted the right of parliament to tax the
colonies in 1764, is true. So did Mr. Otis, in a pamphlet he publifhed the felf-fame year ; from which I have
already taken an extraft. In a pamphlet publifhed in
1765, Mr. Otis tells us, ‘ it is certain that the parliament of
‘ Great-Britain hath a juft, clear, equitable and conftitu-
‘ tional right, power and authority to bind the colonies by
‘ all afts wherein they are named. Every lawyer, nay
‘ every tyro, knows this ; no lefs certain is it that the
‘ parliament of Great-Britain has a juft and *equitable* right,
‘ power and authority, to impofe taxes on the colonies *inter-*
‘ *nal and external, on lands, as well as on trade.* ’ But does
it follow from Governor Bernard’s tranfmitting his principles
of polity to four perfons in England, or from Mr. Otis’s
publifhing to the whole world fimilar principles, that either
the one or the other fuggefted to the miniftry the projeft
of taxing the colonies by aft of parliament ? Hardly,
fuppofing the tranfmiffion and publication had been prior
to the refolution of parliament to that purpofe ; but very
unfortunately for our reafoner, they were both fubfequent
to it, and were the effeft, and not the caufe.

The hiftory of the ftamp-aft is this : At the clofe of the
laft war, which was a native of America, and increafed the
national debt upwards of fixty millions, it was thought by
parliament to be but equitable, that an additional revenue

N   fhould

fhould be raifed in America, towards defraying the neceffary charges of keeping it in a ftate of defence: A refolve
of this nature was paffed, and the colonies made acquainted
with it through their agents, in 1764, that their affemblies might make the neceffary provifion if they would.
The affemblies neglected doing any thing, and the parliament paffed the ftamp-act. There is not fo much as a
colourable pretence, that any American had a hand in the
matter. Had Governor Bernard, Governor Hutchinfon,
or the late Lieutenant-Governor been any way inftrumental
in obtaining the ftamp-act, it is very ftrange that not a
glimpfe of evidence fhould ever have appeared, efpecially
when we confider that their private correfpondence has
been publifhed, letters which were written in the full confidence of unfufpecting friendfhip. The evidence, as Novanglus calls it, is wretchedly deficient as to fixing the
charge upon Governor Bernard ; but even admitting that
Governor Bernard fuggefted to the miniftry the defign of
taxing, there is no kind of evidence to prove that the junto,
as this elegant writer calls the others, approved of it, much
lefs that they employed him to do it. But, fays he, no one
can doubt but that Meffieurs Hutchinfon and Oliver were in
unifon with Governor Bernard, in all his meafures: This
is not a fact; Mr. Hutchinfon diffented from him refpecting the alteration of our charter, and wrote to his friends
in England to prevent it. Whether Governor Bernard
wrote in favour of the ftamp-act being repealed or not, I
cannot fay, but I know that Governor Hutchinfon did,
and have reafon to think his letters had great weight in
turning the fcale, which hung doubtful a long time, in favour of the repeal. Thefe facts are known to many in
the province, whigs as well as tories ; yet fuch was the infatuation that prevailed, that the mob deftroyed his houfe
upon fuppofition that he was the patron of the ftamp-act.
Even in the letters wrote to the late Mr. Whately, we find
him advifing a total repeal of the tea-act. It cannot be
fairly inferred from perfons intimacy or mutual confidence,
that they always approve of each others plans. Meffieurs
Otis, Cufhing, Hancock and Adams were confidential
friends,

friends, and made common caufe equally with the other gentlemen.—May we thence infer, that the three latter hold that the parliament has a juft and *equitable right* to impofe taxes on the colonies? Or, that ' the time may come, when the real intereft of the whole may require an act of parliament to annihilate all our charters?' For thefe alfo are Mr. Otis's words. Or may we lay it down as a principle to reafon from, that thefe gentlemen never difagree refpecting meafures? We know they do often, and very materially too. This writer is unlucky both in his principles and inferences: But where is the evidence refpecting Brigadier Kuggles, Mr Paxton, and the late Judge Ruffel? He does not produce even the fhadow of a fhade. He does not even pretend, that they were in unifon with Governor Bernard in all his meafures. In matters of fmall moment a.man may be allowed to amufe with ingenious fiction; but in perfonal accufation, in matters fo interefting both to the individual and to the public, reafon and candour require fomething more than affertion without proof, declamation without argument, and cenfure without dignity or moderation: This, however, is characteriftic of Novanglus. It is the ftale trick of the whig writers felonioufly to ftab reputations, when their antagonifts are invulnerable in their public conduct.

These gentlemen were all of them, and the furvivors ftill continue to be, friends of the Englifh conftitution, equally tenacious of the privileges of the people and of the prerogative of the crown, zealous advocates for the colonies continuing their conftitutional dependence upon Great-Britain, as they think it no lefs the intereft than the duty of the colonifts, averfe to tyranny and oppreffion in all their forms, and always ready to exert themfelves for the relief of the oppreffed, though they differ materially from the whigs in the mode of obtaining it. They difcharged the duties of the feveral important departments they were called to fill, with equal faithfulnefs and ability; their public fervices gained them the confidence of the people; real merit drew after it popularity; and their principles, firmnefs and popularity rendered them obnoxious to certain perfons

amongft

amongst us, who have long been indulging themselves, in
the hope of rearing up an American common-wealth
upon the ruins of the British constitution. This republican
party is of long standing: they lay however, in a great
measure, dormant for several years. The distrust, jealousy
and ferment, raised by the stamp-act, afforded scope for
action. At first they wore the garb of hypocrisy; they professed to be friends to the British constitution in general,
but claimed some exemptions from their local circumstances; at length they threw off their disguise, and now stand
confessed to the world in their true characters, AMERICAN
REPUBLICANS.—These republicans knew, that it would be
impossible for them to succeed in their darling projects, without first destroying the influence of these adherents to the
constitution: Their only method to accomplish it, was by
publications charged with falshood and scurrility. Notwithstanding the favourable opportunity the stamp-act gave
of imposing upon the ignorant and credulous, I have sometimes been amazed to see, with how little hesitation, some
slovenly baits were swallowed. Sometimes the adherents
to the constitution were called *ministerial tools*; at others,
king, lords and commons, were the tools of *them*: for almost every act of parliament that has been made respecting
America, in the present reign, we are told was draughted
in Boston, or its environs, and only sent to England to run
through the forms of parliament. Such stories, however
improbable, gained credit; even the fictitious bill, for re-
straining marriages and murdering bastard children, met
with some simple enough to think it real. He, that readily
imbibes such absurdities, may claim affinity with the person, mentioned by Mr. Addison, who made it his practice to
swallow a chimera every morning for breakfast. To be
more serious; I pity the weakness of those that are capable
of being thus duped, almost as much as I despise the wretch
that would avail himself of it, to destroy private characters
and the public tranquillity. By such infamous methods,
many of the antient, trusty and skilful pilots, who had
steered the community safely in the most perilous times,
were driven from the helm, and their places occupied by
dif-

different perfons; fome of whom, bankrupts in fortune, bufinefs and fame, are now ftriving to run the fhip on the rocks, that they may have an opportunity of plundering the wreck. The gentlemen, named by Novanglus, have neverthelefs perfevered, with unfhaken conftancy and firmnefs, in their patriotic principles and conduct, through a variety of fortune ; and have, at prefent, the mournful confolation of reflecting, that, had their admonitions and counfels been timely attended to, their country would never have been involved in its prefent calamity.

MASSACHUSETTENSIS.

March 6, 1775.

L E T T E R   XIV.

To the Inhabitants of the Province of Maffachufetts-Bay.

OUR patriotic writers, as they call each other, eftimate the fervices rendered by, and the advantages refulting from, the colonies in Britain, at a high rate; but allow but little, if any, merit in her towards the colonies. Novanglus would perfuade us, that, exclufive of her affiftance in the laft war, we have had but little of her protection, unlefs it was fuch as her name alone afforded. Dr. Franklin, when before the houfe of commons, in 1765, denied, that the late war was entered into for the defence of the people in America. The Pennfylvania Farmer tells us, in his letters, that the war was undertaken folely for the benefit of Great-Britain, and that, however advantageous the fubduing or keeping any of thefe countries, viz. Canada, Nova-Scotia and the Floridas may be to Great-Britain, the acquifition is greatly injurious to thefe colonies; and that the colonies, as conftantly as ftreams tend to the ocean, have been pouring the fruits of all their labours into their mother's lap. Thus, they would induce us to believe, that we derive little or no advantage from Great-Britain, and thence they infer the injuftice, rapacity and cruelty of her conduct towards us. I fully agree with them, that the fervices rendered by the colonies are great and meritorious : The plantations are
add ⸤

additions to the empire of ineftimable value: The American market for Britifh manufactures, the great nurfery for feamen formed by our fhipping, the cultivation of deferts, and our rapid population, are increafing and inexhauftible fources of national wealth and ftrength: I commend thefe patriots for their eftimations of the national advantages accruing from the colonies, as much as I think them deferving of cenfure for depreciating the advantages and benefits that we derive from Britain. A particular enquiry into the protection afforded us, and the commercial advantages refulting to us from the parent-ftate, will go a great way towards conciliating the affections of thofe, whofe minds are at prefent unduly impreffed with different fentiments towards Great-Britain. The inteftine commotions, with which England was convulfed and torn, foon after the emigration of our anceftors, probably prevented that attention being given to them in the earlieft ftages of this colony, that otherwife would have been given. The principal difficulties, that the adventurers met with, after the ftruggle of a few of the firft years were over, were the incurfions of the French and Savages conjointly, or of the latter inftigated and fupported by the former. Upon a reprefentation of this to England, in the time of the interregnum, Acadia, which was then the principal fource of our difquietude, was reduced by an Englifh armament. At the requeft of this colony, in Queen Anne's reign, a fleet of fifteen men of war, befides tranfports, troops, &c. was fent to affift us in an expedition aganft Canada; the fleet fuffered fhipwreck, and the attempt proved abortive. It ought not to be forgotten, that the fiege of Louifbourg, in 1745, by our own forces, was covered by a Britifh fleet of ten fhips, four of 60 guns, one of fifty, and five of 40 guns, befides the Vigilant of fixty-four, which was taken during the fiege, as fhe was attempting to throw fupplies into the garrifon. It is not probable, that the expedition would have been undertaken without an expectation of fome naval affiftance, or that the reduction could have been effected without it. In January, 1754, our affembly, in a meffage to Governor Shirley, prayed him to reprefent to the King,

' that

' that the French had made fuch extraordinary encroachments, and taken fuch meafures, fince the conclufion of the
preceding war, as threatened great danger, and perhaps, in
time, even the intire deftruction of this province, without
the interpofition of his Majefty, notwithftanding any provifion we could make to prevent it :'----' That the French
had erected a fort on the ifthmus of the peninfula near Bay
Vert, in Nova-Scotia, by means of which they maintained
a communication by fea with Canada, St. John's Ifland, and
Louifbourg :—'That near the mouth of St. John's river
the French had poffeffed themfelves of two forts, formerly
built by them, one of which was garrifoned by regular
troops, and had erected another ftrong fort at twenty
leagues up the river, and that thefe encroachments might
prove fatal not only to the eaftern parts of his Majefty's
territories within this province, but alfo, in time, to the
whole of this province, and the reft of his Majefty's territories on this continent :' — ' That whilft the French held
Acadia under the treaty of St. Germain, they fo cut off the
trade of this province, and galled the inhabitants with incurfions into their territories, that OILIVER CROMWELL
found it neceffary, for the fafety of New-England, to
make a defcent by fea into the river of St. John, and dif-
poffefs them of that and all the forts in Acadia. — That
Acadia was reftored to the French by the treaty of Breda,
in 1667 :' — That this colony felt again the fame mifchievous effects from their poffeffing it, infomuch, that after
forming feveral expeditions againft it, the inhabitants were
obliged, in the latter end of the war in Queen Anne's
reign, to reprefent to her Majefty, how deftructive the
poffeffion of the Bay of Fundy and Nova-Scotia, by the
French, was to this province and the Britifh trade ; where-
upon the Britifh miniftry thought it neceffary to fit out a
formal expedition againft that province with Englifh troops,
and a confiderable armament of our own, under General
Nicholfon, by which it was again reduced to the fubjec-
tion of the crown of Great-Britain : — ' That we were
then, viz. in 1754, liable to feel more mifchievous effects
than we had ever yet done, unlefs his Majefty fhould be
pleafed

pleafed to caufe them to be removed.' They alforemon-
ftrated our danger from the encroachments of the French
at Crown Point. — In April, 1754, the Council and Houfe
reprefented, ' That it evidently appeared, that the French
were far advanced in the execution of a plan projected
more than fifty years fince, for the extending their poffeffions from the mouth of the Miffiffippi on the fouth, to Hud-
fon's Bay on the north, for fecuring the vaft body of Indians in that inland country, and for fubjecting the whole
continent to the crown of France:'—' That many circumftances gave them great advantages over us, which,
if not attended to, would foon overbalance our fuperiority
of numbers; and that thefe difadvantages could not be removed without his Majefty's gracious interpofition.'

The Affembly of Virginia, in an addrefs to the King,
reprefented, ' That the endeavour of the French to eftablifh a fettlement upon the frontiers, was a high infult
offered to his Majefty, and, if not timely oppofed with
vigour and refolution, muft be attended with the moft
fatal confequences,' and prayed his Majefty to extend his
royal beneficence towards them.

The commiffioners, who met at Albany the fame year,
reprefented, ' that it was the evident defign of the French
to furround the Britifh colonies; to fortify themfelves on
the back thereof; to take and keep poffeffion of the heads
of all the important rivers; to draw over the Indians to
their intereft, and with the help of fuch Indians, added
to fuch forces as were then arrived, and might afterwards
arrive, or be fent from Europe, to be in a capacity of
making a general attack on the feveral governments; and
if at the fame time a ftrong naval force fhould be fent
from France, there was the utmoft danger that the whole
continent would be fubjected to that crown: and that it
feemed abfolutely neceffary, that fpeedy and effectual meafures fhould be taken to fecure the colonies from the *flavery*
they were threatened with.'

We did not pray in vain. Great-Britain, ever attentive
to the *real grievances* of her colonies, haftened to our relief with maternal fpeed. She covered our feas with her
fhips,

fhips, and fent forth the braveft of her fons to fight our battles. They fought, they bled, and conquered with us. Canada, Nova-Scotia, the Floridas, and all our American foes, were laid at our feet. It was a dear-bought victory; the wilds of America were faturated with the blood of the noble and the brave.

The war, which, at our requeft, was thus kindled in America, fpread through the four quarters of the globe, and obliged Great-Britain to exert her whole force and energy to ftop the rapid progrefs of its devouring flames.

To thefe inftances of actual exertions for our immediate protection and defence, ought to be added the fleets ftationed on our coaft, and the convoys and fecurity afforded to our trade and fifhery in times of war; and her maintaining, in times of peace, fuch a navy and army, as to be always in readinefs to give protection, as exigencies may require; and her ambaffadors, refiding at foreign courts, to watch and give the earlieft intelligence of their motions. By fuch precautions, every part of her wide extended empire enjoys as ample fecurity as human power and policy can afford. Thofe neceffary precautions are fupported at an immenfe expence; and the colonies reap the benefit of them equally with the reft of the empire. To thefe confiderations it fhould likewife be added, that whenever the colonies have exerted themfelves in a war, though in their own defence, to a greater degree than their proportion with the reft of the empire, they have been reimburfed by the parliamentary grants: This was the cafe, in the laft war, with this province.

From this view, which I think is an impartial one, it is evident, that Great-Britain is not lefs attentive to our intereft than her own; and that her fons, who have fettled on new and diftant plantations, are equally dear to her with thofe that cultivate the antient domain, and inhabit the manfion-houfe.

MASSACHUSETTENSIS.

March 13, 1775.

L E T-

L E T T E R XV.

To the Inhabitants of the Province of Maſſachuſetts-Bay.

THE outlines of Britiſh commerce have been heretofore ſketched ; and the intereſts of each part in particular, and of the whole empire conjointly, have been
ſhewn to be the principles by which the grand ſyſtem is
poized and balanced. Whoever will take upon himſelf
the trouble of reading and comparing the ſeveral acts of
trade which reſpect the colonies, will be convinced, that
the cheriſhing their trade and promoting their intereſt have
been the objects of parliamentary attention equally with
thoſe of Britain. He will ſee, that the great council of the
empire has ever eſteemed our proſperity as inſeparable from
the Britiſh ; and if, in ſome inſtances, the colonies have been
reſtricted to the emolument of other parts of the empire,
they in their turn, not excepting England itſelf, have been
alſo reſtricted ſufficiently to reſtore the balance, if not
to cauſe a preponderation in our favour.

Permit me to tranſcribe a page or two from a pamphlet,
written in England, and lately republiſhed here, wherein
this matter is ſtated with great juſtice and accuracy.

‘ The people of England and the American adventur-
‘ ers being ſo differently circumſtanced, it required no
‘ great ſagacity to diſcover, that as there were many com-
‘ modities which America could ſupply on better terms
‘ than they could be raiſed in England, ſo muſt it be
‘ much more for the colonies’ advantage to take others
‘ from England, than attempt to make them themſelves.
‘ The American lands were cheap, covered with woods,
‘ and abounded with native commodities. The firſt at-
‘ tention of the ſettlers was neceſſarily engaged in cutting
‘ down the timber, and clearing the ground for culture ;
‘ for before they had ſupplied themſelves with proviſions,
‘ and had hands to ſpare from agriculture, it was impoſ-
‘ ſible they could ſet about manufacturing. England,
‘ therefore, undertook to ſupply them with manufactures,
‘ and either purchaſed herſelf or found markets for the

‘ timber

' timber, the colonists cut down upon their lands, or the
' fish they caught upon their coasts. It was soon disco-
' vered that the tobacco plant was a native of, and flou-
' rished in, Virginia. It had been also planted in Eng-
' land, and was found to delight in the soil. The legil-
' lature however, wisely and equitably confidering that
' England had variety of products, and Virginia had no
' other to buy her neceffaries with, passed an act prohi-
' biting the people of England from planting tobacco,
' and thereby giving the monopoly of that plant to the
' colonies. As the inhabitants increased, and the lands
' became more cultivated, further and new advantages
' were thrown in the way of the American colonies.
' All foreign markets, as well as Great-Britain, were
' open for their timber and provisions; and the British
' West-India islands were prohibited from purchasing
' those commodities from any other than them. And
' fince England has found itself in danger of wanting a
' supply of timber, and it has been judged neceffary to con-
' fine the export from America to Great-Britain and
' Ireland, full and ample indemnity has been given to the
' colonies for the lofs of a choice of markets in Europe, by
' very large bounties paid out of the revenue of Great-
' Britain, upon the importation of American timber. And
' as a further encouragement and reward to them for clear-
' ing their lands, bounties are given upon tar and pitch,
' which are made from their decayed and ulelefs trees;
' and the very ashes of their lops and branches are made
' of value by the late bounty on American potashes.
' The soil and climate of the northern colonies having
' been found well adapted to the culture of flax and
' hemp, bounties, equal to half the first coft of those
' commodities, have been granted by parliament, payable
' out of the British revenue, upon their importation in-
' to Great-Britain. The growth of rice in the southern
' colonies has been greatly encouraged, by prohibiting
' the importation of that grain into the British domini-
' ons from other parts, and allowing it to be tranfported
' from the colonies to the foreign territories in America,

and

' and even to the fouthern parts of Europe. Indigo has
' been nurtured in thofe colonies by great parliamentary
' bounties, which have been long paid upon the importa-
' tion into Great-Britain, and of late are allowed to re-
' main, even when it is carried out again to foreign mar-
' kets. Silk and wine have alfo been objects of parlia-
' mentary munificence, and will one day probably be-
' come confiderable American products, under that en-
' couragement. In which of thefe inftances, it may be
' demanded, has the legiflature fhewn itfelf partial to the
' people of England and unjuft to the colonies? Or where-
' in have the colonies been injured? We hear much of
' the reftraints under which the trade of the colonies is laid
' by acts of parliament for the advantage of Great-Britain,
' but the reftraints under which the people of Great-Britain
' are laid by acts of parliament, for the advantage of the
' colonies, are carefully kept out of fight;---and yet, upon
' a comparifon, the one will be found full as grievous as
' the other.---For is it a greater hardfhip on the colonies,
' to be confined in fome inftances to the markets of Great-
' Britain for the fale of their commodities, than it is on the
' people of Great-Britain to be obliged to buy the commo-
' dities from them only? If the ifland colonies are obliged
' to give the people of Great-Britain the pre-emption of
' their fugar and coffee; is it not a greater hardfhip on the
' people of Great-Britain to be reftrained from purchafing
' fugar and coffee from other countries, where they could
' get them much cheaper than the colonies make them pay
' for them? Could not our manufacturers have indigo
' much better and cheaper from France and Spain than
' from Carolina? And yet is there not a duty impofed by
' acts of parliament on French and Spanifh indigo, that it
' may come to our manufacturers at a dearer rate than Ca-
' rolina indigo, though a bounty is alfo given out of *the*
' *money* of the people of England to the Carolina planter,
' to enable him to fell his indigo upon a *par* with the French
' and Spanifh? But the inftance which has been already
' taken notice of, the act which prohibits the culture of
' the tobacco plant in Great-Britain or Ireland, is ftill more
' in

' in point, and a more ſtriking proof of the juſtice and im-
' partiality of the ſupreme legiſlature : for what reſtraints,
' let me aſk, are the colonies laid under, which bear ſuch
' ſtrong marks of hardſhip, as prohibiting the farmers in
' Great-Britain and Ireland from raiſing, upon their own
' lands, a product which is become almoſt a neceſſary of
' life to them and their families ?   And this moſt extraor-
' dinary reſtraint is laid upon them, for the avowed and ſole
' purpoſe of giving Virginia and Maryland a monopoly of
' that commodity, and obliging the people of Great-Bri-
' tain and Ireland to buy all the tobacco they conſume,
' from them, at the prices they think fit to ſell it for.   The
' annals of no country, that ever planted colonies, can pro-
' duce ſuch an inſtance as this of regard and kindneſs to their
' colonies, and of reſtraint upon the inhabitants of the mo-
' ther-country for their advantage. Nor is there any reſtraint
' laid upon the inhabitants of the colonies in return, which
' carries in it ſuch great appearance of hardſhip, although the
' people of Great-Britain and Ireland have, from their regard
' and affection to the colonies, ſubmitted to it without a mur-
' mur for near a century.'   For a more particular inquiry,
let me recommend the peruſal of the pamphlet itſelf, and
alſo of another pamphlet lately publiſhed, entitled, ' the
' advantages which America derives from her commerce,
' connection and dependence on Great-Britain.'

A calculation has lately been made both of the amount
of the revenue ariſing from the duties with which our trade
is at preſent charged, and of the bounties and encouragement paid out of the Britiſh revenue upon articles of American produce imported into England ; *and the latter is
found to exceed the former more than four-fold.*   This
does not look like a partiality to our diſadvantage :—
However, there is no ſurer method of determining whether
the colonies have been oppreſſed by the laws of trade and
revenue, than by obſerving their effects.

From what ſource has the *wealth* of the colonies flowed ?
Whence is it derived ?   Not from agriculture only.   Exclu-
ſive of commerce, the coloniſts would this day have been a
poor people, poſſeſſed of little more than the neceſſaries for
ſup-

supporting life ; of courfe their numbers would be few ; for population always keeps pace with the ability of maintaining a family : there would have been but little or no refort of ftrangers here ; the arts and fciences would have made but fmall progrefs ; the inhabitants would rather have degenerated into a ftate of ignorance and barbarity. Or had Great-Britain laid fuch reftrictions upon our trade, as our patriots would induce us to believe, that is, had we been pouring the fruits of all our labour into the lap of our parent, and been enriching her by the fweat of our brow, without receiving an equivalent ; the patrimony derived from our anceftors muft have dwindled from little to lefs, till their pofterity fhould have fuffered a general bankruptcy.

But how different are the effects of our connection with, and fubordination to Britain? They are too ftrongly marked to efcape the moft carelefs obferver. Our merchants are opulent, and our yeomanry in eafier circumftances than the nobleffe of fome ftates : Population is fo rapid as to double the number of inhabitants in the fhort period of twenty-five years : Cities are fpringing up in the depths of the wildernefs : Schools, colleges, and even univerfities, are interfperfed through the continent : Our country abounds with foreign refinements, and flows with exotic luxuries. Thefe are infallible marks, not only of *opulence*, but of *freedom*. The reclufe may fpeculate— the envious repine—the difaffected calumniate ;—all thefe may combine to create fears and jealoufies in the minds of the multitude, and keep them in alarm from the beginning to the end of the year ; but fuch evidence as this muft for ever carry conviction with it to the minds of the difpaffionate and judicious.

Where are the traces of flavery, that our patriots would terrify us with ? The effects of flavery are as glaring and obvious in thofe countries that are curfed with its abode, as the effects of war, peftilence, or famine. Our land is not difgraced by the wooden fhoes of France, or the uncombed hair of Poland : We have neither racks nor inquifitions, tortures nor affaffinations : The mildnefs of

our

our criminal jurifprudence is proverbial, ' *a man muft have* ' *many friends to get hanged in New-England.*' Who has been arbitrarily imprifoned, diffeized of his freehold, or defpoiled of his goods ? Each peafant, that is induftrious, may acquire an eftate, enjoy it in his life-time, and at his death tranfmit a fair inheritance to his pofterity. The proteftant religion is eftablifhed, as far as human laws can eftablifh it. My dear friends, let me afk each one, whether he has not enjoyed every blefling that is in the power of civil government to beftow ? And yet the parliament has, from the earlieft days of the colonies, claimed the lately controverted right both of legiflation and taxation, and for more than a century has been in the exercife of it. There is no grievous exercife of that right at this day, unlefs the meafures taken to prevent our revolting may be called grievances. Are we then to rebel, left there fhould be grievances ? Are we to take up arms and make war againft our parent, left that parent, contrary to the experience of a century and a half, contrary to her own genius, inclination, affection, and intereft, fhould treat us or our pofterity as baftards and not as fons, and inftead of protecting fhould *enflave* us ? The annals of the world have not yet been deformed with a fingle inftance of fo unnatural, fo caufelefs, fo wanton, fo wicked, a rebellion.

There is but a ftep between you and ruin ; and fhould our patriots fucceed in their endeavours to urge you on to take that ftep, and hoftilities actually commence, New-England will ftand recorded a fingular monument of human folly and wickednefs. I beg leave to tranfcribe a little from the Farmer's letters :—' Good Heaven ! Shall ' a total oblivion of former tendernefles and bleflings be ' fpread over the minds of a good and wife people, by the ' fordid arts of intriguing men, who, covering their felfifh ' projects under pretences of public good, firft enrage ' their country-men into a frenzy of paffion which they ' themfelves have excited ?' When cool difpaffionate pofterity fhall confider the affectionate intercourfe, the reciprocal benefits, and the unfufpecting confidence, that have fubfifted between thefe colonies and their parent

ftate

ftate for fuch a length of time ; they will execrate, with the bittereft curfes, the infamous memory of thofe men, whofe ambition, unneceffarily, wantonly, cruelly, firft opened the fources of civil difcord.

MASSACHUSETTENSIS.
March 20, 1775.

L E T T E R XVI.

To the Inhabitants of the Province of Maffachufetts-Bay.

OUR patriots exclaim, That humble and reafonable petitions from the reprefentatives of the people have been frequently treated with contempt. This is as virulent a libel upon his Majefty's government, as falfhood and in-genuity combined could fabricate. Our humble and rea-fonable petitions have not only been ever gracioufly receiv-ed, when the eftablifhed mode of exhibiting them has been obferved, but generally granted. Applications of a differ-ent kind have been treated with negleƈt, though not al-ways with the contempt they deferved. Thefe either ori-ginated in illegal affemblies, and could not be received without implicitly countenancing fuch enormities, or con-tained fuch matter, and were conceived in fuch terms, as to be at once an infult to his Majefty and a libel on his government. Inftead of being decent remonftrances againft real grievances, or prayers for their removal, they were infidious attempts to wreft from the crown, or the fupreme legiflature, their inherent, unalienable prerogatives or rights.

We have a recent inftance of this kind of petition, in the application of the continental congrefs to the King, which ftarts with thefe words : ' A ftanding army has been kept in thefe colonies ever fince the conclufion of the late war, *without the confent of our affemblies.*' This is a denial of the King's authority to ftation his military forces in fuch parts of the empire, as his Majefty may judge expedient for the common fafety. They might with equal propriety have advanced one ftep further, and denied its being a prerogative of the crown to declare war, or conclude a

peace

peace by which the colonies should be affected, without the consent of our assemblies. Such petitions carry the marks of death in their faces, as they cannot be granted but by surrendering some constitutional right at the same time; and therefore they afford grounds for suspicion at least, that they were never intended to be granted, but to irritate and provoke the power petitioned to. It is one thing to remonstrate the inexpediency or inconveniency of a particular act of the prerogative, and another to deny the existence of the prerogative. It is one thing to complain of the inutility or hardship of a particular act of parliament, and quite another to deny the authority of parliament to make any act. Had our patriots confined themselves to the former, they would have acted a part conformable to the character they assumed, and merited the encomiums they arrogate.

There is not one act of parliament that respects us, but would have been repealed upon the legislators being convinced that it was oppressive; and scarcely one, but would have shared the same fate, upon a representation of its being generally disgustful to America. But, by adhering to the latter, our politicians have ignorantly or wilfully betrayed their country. Even when Great-Britain has relaxed in her measures, or appeared to recede from her claims, instead of manifestations of gratitude, our politicians have risen in their demands, and sometimes to such a degree of insolence, as to lay the British government under a necessity of persevering in its measures to preserve its honor.

It was my intention, when I began these papers, to have minutely examined the proceedings of the continental congress; as the delegates appear to me to have given their country a deeper wound, than any of their predecessors had inflicted, and I pray God it may not prove an incurable one; but am in some measure anticipated by Grotius, Phileareine, and the many pamphlets that have been published, and shall therefore confine my observations to some of its most striking and characteristic features.

A congress or convention of committees from the several colonies, constitutionally appointed by the supreme autho-

P   rity

rity of the state, or by the several provincial legislatures, amenable to and controlable by the power that convened them, would be salutary in many suppofable cafes: Such was the convention of 1754; but a congrefs, otherwife appointed, muft be an unlawful affembly, wholly incompatible with the conftitution, and dangerous in the extreme; more efpecially as fuch affemblies will ever chiefly confift of the moft violent partizans. The Prince or Sovereign, as fome writers call the fupreme authority of a ftate, is fufficiently ample and extenfive to provide a remedy for every wrong in all poffible emergencies and contingencies; confequently, a power that is not derived from fuch authority, fpringing up in a ftate, muft encroach upon it; and in proportion as the ufurpation inlarges itfelf, the rightful prince muft be diminifhed: indeed they cannot long fubfift together, but muft continually militate till one or the other be deftroyed. Had the continental congrefs confifted of committees from the feveral houfes of affembly, although deftitute of the confent of the feveral governors, they would have had fome appearance of authority; but many of them were appointed by other committees, as illegally conftituted as themfelves. However, at fo critical and delicate a juncture, Great-Britain being alarmed with an apprehenfion that the colonies were aiming at independence on the one hand, and the colonies apprehenfive of grievous impofitions and exactions from Great-Britain on the other; many real patriots imagined that a congrefs might be eminently ferviceable, as they might prevail on the Boftonians to make reftitution to the Eaft-India company, might ftill the commotions in this province, remove any ill-founded apprehenfions refpecting the colonies, and propofe fome plan for a cordial and permanent reconciliation, which might be adopted by the feveral affemblies, and make its way through them to the fupreme legiflature. Placed in this point of light, many good men viewed it with an indulgent eye; and tories, as well as whigs, bade the delegates God fpeed.

The path of duty was too plain to be overlooked; but unfortunately fome of the moft influential of the members were

were the very perfons, that had been the *wilful* caufe of the
evils they were expected to remedy. Fifhing in troubled
waters had long been their bufinefs and delight; and they
deprecated nothing more than that the ftorm, they had
blown up, fhould fubfide. They were old in intrigue,
and would have figured in a conclave. The fubtilty, hy-
pocrify, cunning and chicanery, habitual to fuch men,·
were practifed with as much fuccefs in this, as they had
been before in other popular affemblies.

Some of the members, of the firft rate abilities and
characters, endeavoured to confine the deliberations and
refolves of the congrefs to the defign of its inftitution,
which was ' to reftore peace, harmony and mutual confi-
' dence,' but were obliged to fubmit to the intemperate
zeal of fome, and at length were fo circumvented and
wrought upon by the artifice and duplicity of others, as to
lend the fanction of their names to fuch meafures as they
condemned in their hearts. See a pamphlet publifhed
by one of the delegates intitled, *A candid examination,*
&c.

The Congrefs could not be ignorant of what every body
elfe knew, that their appointment was repugnant to, and
inconfiftent with, every idea of government, and therefore
they wifely determined to deftroy it. Their firft effay that
tranfpired, and which was matter of no lefs grief to the
friends of our country than of triumph to its enemies, was
the ever-memorable refolve approving and adopting the
Suffolk refolves, thereby undertaking to give a continental
fanction to a forcible oppofition to acts of parliament,
fhutting up the courts of juftice, and thereby abrogating
all human laws, feizing the King's provincial revenue,
raifing forces in oppofition to the King's, and all the tumultuary violence, with which this unhappy province has
been rent afunder.

This fixed the complexion and marked the character of
the congrefs. We were therefore but little furprized when
it was announced, that, as far as was in their power, they
had difmembered the colonies from the parent-country.
This they did by refolving, that ' the colonifts are entitled

P 2   ' to

' to an exclufive power of legiflation in their feveral pro-
' vincial legiflatures.' This ftands in its full force, and is
an abfolute denial of the authority of parliament refpecting
the colonies.

Their fubjoining that ' *from neceffity* they confent to the
' *operation* (not the authority) of fuch acts of the *Britiſh*
' parliament as *are* (not fhall be) *bonâ fide* reftrained to ex-
' ternal commerce,' is fo far from weakening their firſt
principle that it ftrengthens it, and extends to the acts
of trade   This refolve is a manifeſt revolt from the Britiſh
empire.—Confiftent with it, is their overlooking the fupreme legiflature, and addreffing the inhabitants of Great-
Britain, in the ftyle of a manifeſto, in which they flatter,
complain, coax, and threaten alternately : Their prohibiting all commercial intercourfe between the two countries ;
with equal propriety and juſtice, the congrefs might have
declared war againſt Great-Britain, and they intimate that
they might juſtly do it, and actually fhall, if the meaſures
already taken prove ineffectual ; for in the addrefs to the
colonies, after attempting to enrage their countrymen, by
every colouring and heightening in the power of language,
to the utmoſt pitch of frenzy, they fay, ' the ſtate of theſe
' colonies would certainly juſtify *other* meaſures than we
' have adviſed ; we were inclined to offer *once more* to his
' *Majeſty* the petition of his faithful and oppreſſed ſubjects
' in America ;' and then they admoniſh the coloniſts to ' ex-
' tend their views to *mournful events*, and to be in all refpects
' prepared for every contingency.'

This is treating Great-Britain as an alien-enemy ; and if
Great-Britain be fuch, it is juftifiable by the law of nations :
but their attempt to alienate the affections of the inhabitants of the new conquered province of Quebec from his
majefty's government, is altogether unjuſtifiable, even upon
that principle.   In the truly jefuitical addrefs to the Canadians, the congrefs endeavour to feduce them from their allegiance, and to prevail on them to join the confederacy.
After infinuating that they had been tricked, duped, oppreffed and enflaved by the Quebec bill, the congrefs exclaim, ' Why this degrading diftinction ? Have not Cana-
' dians

' dians fenfe enough to attend to any other public affairs
' than gathering ftones at one place and piling them up in
' another ? Unhappy people! who are not only injured,
' but *infulted.*' 'Such a treacherous ingenuity has been
' exerted in drawing up the code lately offered you, that
' every fentence, beginning with a benevolent pretenfion,
' concludes with a deftructive power ; and the fubftance
' of the whole, divefted of its fmooth words, is, that the
' *crown* and its minifters fhall be as abfolute throughout
' your extended province, as the *defpots of Afia or Africa.*
' We defy you, cafting your view upon every fide, to dif-
' cover a fingle circumftance promifing, from any quarter,
' the fainteft hope of liberty to you or your pofterity, but
' from an entire adoption into the union of thefe colonies.'
The treachery of the congrefs in this addrefs is the more flagrant, by the Quebec bill's having been adapted to the genius and manners of the Canadians, formed upon their own
petition, and received with every teftimonial of gratitude.
The public tranquillity has been often difturbed by trea-
fonable plots and confpiracies. Great Britain has been repeatedly deluged by the blood of its flaughtered citizens,
and fhaken to its centre by rebellion.—To offer fuch aggravated infult to Britifh government, was referved for the
grand continental congrefs. None but ideots or madmen,
could fuppofe fuch meafures had a tendency to reftore ' union
' and harmony between Great-Britain and the colonies:'
Nay! The very demands of the congrefs evince, that *that*
was not in their intention.—Inftead of confining themfelves
to thofe acts, which occafioned the mifunderftanding, they
demand a repeal of fourteen, and bind the colonies by a
law not to trade with Great-Britain until that fhall be done.
Then, and not before, the colonifts are to treat Great-Britain as an alien friend, and in no other light is the parent-
country ever after to be viewed ; for the parliament is to
furceafe enacting laws to refpect us for ever. Thefe demands are fuch as cannot be complied with, confiftent with
either the honor or intereft of the empire, and are therefore infuperable obftacles to a union by means of the congrefs.

The

The delegates erecting themselves into the States-General or supreme legiflature of all the colonies from *Nova-Scotia* to *Georgia*, do not leave a doubt refpecting their aiming, in good earneft, at independency : This they did by enacting laws.—Although they recognize the authority of the feveral provincial legiflatures, yet they confider their own authority as paramount or fupreme ; otherwife they would not have acted decifively, but fubmitted their plans to the final determination of the affemblies. Sometimes indeed they ufe the terms *requeft* and *recommend* ; at others they fpeak in the ftyle of authority.—Such is the refolve of the 27th of September : ' Refolved, from and after the
' firft day of December next, there be no importation into
' Britifh America from Great-Britain or Ireland of any
' goods, wares, or merchandize whatfoever, or from any
' other place of any fuch goods, wares or merchandize
' as fhall have been exported from Great-Britain or Ire-
' land, and that no fuch goods, wares or merchandize, im-
' ported after the faid firft day of December next, be ufed
' or purchafed.' October 15, the congrefs refumed the confideration of the plan for carrying into effect, the non-importation, &c. October 20, the plan is compleated, determined upon, and ordered to be fubfcribed by all the members : They call it an affociation, but it has all the conftituent parts of a law. They begin,—
' We his Majefty's moft loyal fubjects, the delegates of the
' feveral colonies of, &c. deputed to *reprefent them* in a
' continental congrefs,' and agree for themfelves and the inhabitants of the feveral colonies whom they reprefent, not to import, export, or confume, &c. as alfo to obferve feveral fumptuary regulations under certain penalties and forfeitures, and that a committee be chofen in every county, city, and town, by thofe who are qualified to vote as reprefentatives in the legiflature, to fee that the affociation be obferved and kept, and to punifh the violaters of it ; and, afterwards, ' recommended it to the provincial
' conventions, and to the committees in the refpective
' colonies, to eftablifh fuch further regulations as they may
' think proper, for carrying into execution the affociation.'

Here

Here we find the congrefs enacting laws,—that is, eftablifhing, as the reprefentatives of the people, certain rules
of conduct to be obferved and kept by all the inhabitants
of thefe colonies, under certain pains and penalties,—fuch
as mafters of veffels being difmiffed from their employment;—goods to be feized and fold at auction, and the
firft coft only returned to the proprietor, a different appropriation made of the overplus;—perfons being ftigmatized in the gazette, as enemies to their country, and excluded the benefits of fociety, &c.

The congrefs feem to have been apprehenfive, that fome
fqueamifh people might be ftartled at their affuming the
powers of legiflation, and therefore, in the former part of
their affociation, fay, they bind themfelves and conftituents under the facred ties of virtue, honor, and love to
their country, afterwards eftablifh penalties and forfeitures,
and conclude by folemnly binding themfelves and conftituents under the ties aforefaid, which include them all.—
This looks like artifice:—But they might have fpared
themfelves that trouble, for every law is or ought to be
made under the facred ties of virtue, honor, and a love to
the country, expreffed or implied, though the penal fanction be alfo neceffary. In fhort, were the colonies diftinct
ftates, and the powers of legiflation vefted in delegates
thus appointed, their affociation would be as good a form
of enacting laws as could be devifed.

By their affuming the powers of legiflation, the congrefs
have not only fuperfeded our provincial legiflatures, but
have excluded every idea of monarchy; and, not content
with the havock already made in our conftitution, in the
plenitude of their power, they have appointed another
congrefs to be held in May.

Thofe that have attempted to eftablifh new fyftems have
generally taken care to be confiftent with themfelves. Let
us compare the feveral parts of the continental proceedings with each other.

The delegates call themfelves and conftituents, ‘ his
‘ Majefty’s moft loyal fubjects;’ his Majefty’s moft faithful fubjects affirm, that the colonifts are entitled ‘ to all
‘ the

' the immunities and privileges granted and confirmed to
' them by royal charters,' declare that they ' wish not a
' diminution of the prerogative, nor solicit the grant of any
' new right or favour,' and that they ' shall always care-
' fully and zealously endeavour to support his royal autho-
' rity, and our connection with Great-Britain ;'—yet they
deny the King's prerogative to station troops in the colonies,
disown him in the capacity in which he granted the provincial charters; disclaim the authority of the King in
parliament; and undertake to enact and execute laws,
without any authority derived from the crown. This is
dissolving all connection between the colonies and the
crown, and giving us a new King, altogether incompre-
hensible, not indeed from the infinity of his attributes, but
from a privation of every royal prerogative, and not leaving
even the semblance of a connection with Great-Britain.

They declare, that the colonists ' are entitled to all the
' rights, liberties and immunities of free and natural born
' subjects within the realm of England,' and ' all the be-
' nefits secured to the subject by the English constitution,'
but disclaim all obedience to British government ; — in
other words, they claim the protection, and disclaim the
allegiance. They remonstrate as a grievance, that ' both
' houses of parliament have resolved, that the colonists may
' be tried in England for offences alledged to have been
' committed in America, by virtue of a statute passed in
' the thirty-fifth year of Henry the eighth ;'—and yet resolve, that they are entitled to the benefit of such English
statutes as existed at the time of their colonization, and
are applicable to their several local and other circumstances. They resolve that the colonists are entitled to a
free and *exclusive* power of legislation in their several provincial assemblies ;—yet undertake to *legislate in congress.*

The immutable laws of nature, the principles of the
English constitution, and our several charters, are the basis
upon which they pretend to found themselves, and complain more especially of being deprived of trials by juries ;
—but establish ordinances incompatible with either the
laws of nature, the English constitution, or our charter;
—and

—and appoint committees to punifh the violaters of them, not only without a jury, but even without a form of trial.

They repeatedly complain of the Roman Catholic reliligion being eftablifhed in Canada, and, in their addrefs to the Canadians, afk, ' if liberty of confcience be offered ' them *in their religion* by the Quebec bill,' and anfwer, ' no ; God gave it to you, and the temporal powers, with ' which you have been and are connected, firmly ftipulated ' for your enjoyment of it. If laws *divine* and *human* could ' fecure it againft the defpotic caprices of wicked men, it ' was fecured before.'

They fay to the people of Great-Britain, ' place us in ' the fame fituation that we were in at the clofe of the laft ' war, and our harmony will be reftored.' Yet fome of the principal grievances, which are to be redreffed, exifted long before that æra, viz. the King's keeping a ftanding army in the colonies ;—judges of admiralty receiving their fees, &c. from the effects condemned by themfelves ;— councillors holding commiffions during pleafure; exercifing legiflative authority ;—and the capital grievance of all, the parliament claiming and exercifing over the colonies a right of taxation. However, the *wifdom* of the grand continental congrefs may reconcile thefe feeming inconfiftences.

Had the delegates been appointed to devife means to irritate and enrage the inhabitants of the two countries, againft each other, beyond a poffibility of reconciliation, to abolifh our equal fyftem of jurifprudence, and eftablifh a judicatory as arbitrary as the Roman inquifition, to perpetuate animofities among ourfelves, to reduce thoufands from affluence to poverty and indigence—to injure Great-Britain, Ireland, the Weft-Indies and thefe colonies—to attempt a revolt from the authority of the empire—and finally to draw down upon the colonies the whole vengeance of Great-Britain ;—more promifing means to effect the whole could not have been devifed than thofe the congrefs have adopted.—Any deviation from their plan would have been treachery to their conftituents, and an abufe of the truft and confidence repofed in them. Some idolaters have

attributed

attributed to the congrefs the collected wifdom of the continent. It is nearer the truth to fay, that every particle of difaffection, petulance, ingratitude and difloyalty, that for ten years paft have been fcattered through the continent, were united and confolidated in them. Are thefe thy Gods, O Ifrael!

MASSACHUSETTENSIS.

March 27, 1775.

L E T T E R   XVII.

To the Inhabitants of the Province of Maffachufetts-Bay.

THE advocates for the oppofition to parliament, often remind us of the rights of the people, repeat the Latin adage, *vox populi vox Dei*, and tell us, that government, in the dernier refort, is in the people :—they chime away melodioufly, and, to render their mufic more ravifhing, tell us, that thefe are *revolution* principles. I hold the rights of the people to be facred, and revere the principles that have eftablifhed the fucceffion to the imperial crown of Great-Britain in the line of the illuftrious houfe of Brunfwick ; but the difficulty lies in applying them to the caufe of the whigs, *hic labor, hoc opus eft* ; for admitting, that the collective body of the people, that are fubject to the Britifh empire, have an inherent right to change their form of government, or race of Kings ; it does not follow, that the inhabitants of a fingle province or of a number of provinces, or any given part under a majority of the whole empire, have fuch a right. By admitting that the lefs may rule or fequefter themfelves from the greater, we unhinge all government. Novanglus has accufed me of traducing the people of this province : I deny the charge. Popular demagogues always call themfelves *the people*, and, when their own meafures are cenfured, cry out, the people, the people are abufed and infulted. He fays, that I once entertained different fentiments from thofe now advanced : I did not write to exculpate myfelf : If through ignorance, or inadvertency, I have heretofore contributed, in any degree, to the

form-

forming that deſtructive ſyſtem of politics that is now in vogue, I was under the greater obligation thus publicly to expoſe its errors, and point out its pernicious tendency. He ſuggeſts, that I write from ſordid motives: I deſpiſe the imputation. I have written my real ſentiments, not to ſerve a party (for as he juſtly obſerves, I have ſometimes quarrelled with my friends) but to ſerve the public ; nor would I injure my country to inherit all the treaſures that avarice and ambition ſigh for. Fully convinced that our calamities were chiefly created by the leading whigs, and that a perſevering in the ſame meaſures, that gave riſe to our troubles, would complete our ruin ; I have written freely. It is painful to me to give offence to an individual, but I have not ſpared the ruinous policy of my brother or my friend,—they are both far advanced.—Truth from its own energy will finally prevail, but, to have ſpeedy effect, it muſt ſometimes be accompanied with ſeverity. *The terms whig and tory have been adopted according to the arbitrary uſe of them in this province, but they rather ought to be reverſed ; an American tory is a ſupporter of our excellent conſtitution, and an American whig is a ſubverter of it.*

Novanglus abuſes me for ſaying, that the whigs aim at independence. The writer from Hampſhire county is my advocate : He frankly aſſerts the independency of the colonies without any reſerve, and is the only conſiſtent writer I have met with on that ſide of the queſtion ; for, by ſeparating us from the King as well as the parliament, he is under no neceſſity of contradicting himſelf. Novanglus ſtrives to hide the inconſiſtences of his hypotheſis, under a huge pile of learning. Surely he is not to learn, that arguments drawn from obſolete maxims, raked out of the ruins of the feudal ſyſtem, or from principles of abſolute monarchy, will not conclude to the preſent conſtitution of government: When he has finiſhed his eſſays, he may expect ſome particular remarks upon them. I ſhould not have taken the trouble of writing theſe letters, had I not been ſatisfied that real and permanent good would accrue to this province, and indeed to all the colonies, from a ſpeedy

Q 2 change

change of meafures. Public juftice and generofity are no
lefs characteriftic of the Englifh, than their private honefty
and hofpitality. The total repeal of the ftamp-act, and the
partial repeal of the act impofing duties on paper, &c. may
convince us, that the nation has no difpofition to injure us.
We are bleffed with a King that reflects honor upon a crown:
He is fo far from being avaricious, that he has relinquifhed
a part of his revenue; and fo far from being tyrannical, that
he has generoufly furrendered part of his prerogative for the
fake of freedom. His court is fo far from being tinctured
with diffipation, that the palace is rather an academy of the
literati; and the royal pair are as exemplary in every private virtue, as they are exalted in their ftations. We have
only to ceafe contending with the fupreme legiflature refpecting its authority, with the King refpecting his prerogatives, and with Great-Britain refpecting our fubordination; to difmifs our illegal committees, difband our forces,
defpife the thraldom of *arrogant congreffes*, and fubmit to
conftitutional government; to be happy.

Many appear to confider themfelves as *procul à Jove à
fulmine procul*, and, becaufe we never have experienced any
feverity from Great-Britain, think it impoffible that we
fhould. The Englifh nation will bear much from its friends,
but whoever has read its hiftory muft know, that there is a
line that cannot be paffed with impunity: It is not the fault
of our patriots if that line be not already paffed: They have
demanded of Great-Britain more than fhe can grant confiftent with her honor, her intereft, or our own, and are
now brandifhing the fword of defiance.

Do you expect to conquer in war? War is no longer a
fimple but an intricate fcience, not to be learned from books,
or two or three campaigns, but from long experience. You
need not be told, that his Majefty's Generals, Gage and Hal-
dimand, are poffeffed of every talent requifite to great com-
manders, matured by long experience in many parts of the
world, and ftand high in military fame; that many of the
officers have been bred to arms from their infancy, and a
large

large proportion of the army, *now* here, have already reaped
immortal honors in the iron harveſt of the field.—Alas!
My friends, you have nothing to oppoſe to this force, but
a militia unuſed to ſervice, impatient of command, and deſtitute of reſources. Can your officers depend upon the
privates, or the privates upon the officers? Your war can
be but little more than mere tumultuary rage: And beſides, there is an awful diſparity between troops that fight
the battles of their Sovereign, and thoſe that follow the
ſtandard of rebellion. Theſe reflections may arreſt you in
an hour that you think not of, and come too late to ſerve
you. Nothing ſhort of a miracle could gain you one battle; but could you deſtroy all the Britiſh troops that are
now here, and burn the men of war that command our
coaſt, it would be but the beginning of ſorrow; and yet,
without a deciſive battle, one campaign would ruin you.
This province does not produce its neceſſary proviſion,when
the huſbandman can purſue his calling without moleſtation:
What then muſt be your condition, when the demand ſhall
be increaſed and the reſource in a manner cut off?—Figure to yourſelves, what muſt be your diſtreſs ſhould your
wives and children be driven from ſuch places, as theKing's
troops ſhall occupy, into the interior parts of the province,
and they, as well as you, be deſtitute of ſupport. I take
no pleaſure in painting theſe ſcenes of diſtreſs. The whigs
affect to divert you from them by ridicule;—but ſhould
war commence, you can expect nothing but its ſeverities.
Might I hazard an opinion, but few of your leaders ever
intended to engage in hoſtilities; but they may have rendered inevitable what they intended for intimidation. Thoſe
that unſheath the ſword of rebellion may throw away the
ſcabbard; they cannot be treated with while in arms; and
if they lay them down, they are in no other predicament
than conquered rebels. The conquered in other wars do
not forfeit the rights of men, nor all the rights of citizens,
even their bravery is rewarded by a generous victor; far
different is the caſe of a routed rebel hoſt. My dear countrymen, you have before you, at your election, peace or
war,

war, happinefs or mifery. May the God of our forefathers direct you in the way that leads to peace and happinefs, before your feet ftumble on the dark mountains,—before the evil days come, wherein you fhall fay, We have no pleafure in them.

MASSACHUSETTENSIS.

April 3, 1775.

THE END.

Printed and fold by J. MATHEWS,

Americans againft Liberty : or an Effay on the Nature and Principles of true Freedom, fhewing that the Defigns and Conduct of the Americans tend only to Tyranny and Slavery. Price *One Shilling and Six-pence.*

LI'